W9-AAE-562

THE WINE CHRONICLES

© 2002 by Greg Moore
All rights reserved under the Pan-American and International Copyright
Conventions
Printed in China

This book may not be reproduced in whole or in part, in any form or by
any means, electronic or mechanical, including photocopying, recording, or
by any information storage and retrieval system now known or hereafter
invented, without written permission from the publisher.

9   8   7   6   5   4   3   2   1
Digit on the right indicates the number of this printing

ISBN 0-7624-1358-1

Picture research by Susan Oyama
Cover illustration by Christopher Wormell
Cover and interior design by Dustin Summers
Edited by Elizabeth Shiflett
Typography: Bembo, Trade Gothic

This book may be ordered by mail from the publisher.
Please include $2.50 for postage and handling.
But try your bookstore first!

Running Press Book Publishers
125 South Twenty-second Street
Philadelphia, Pennsylvania 19103-4399

Visit us on the web!
www.runningpress.com

Picture Credits:
© 2002 Christopher Wormell: cover and
spot illustrations
© Corbis: p. 30
© David Fields: pp. 26–27

H. Armstrong Roberts:
© David Lada: p. 6
© Rolf Richardson: p. 10
© Blackfan: p. 12
© David Carriere: p. 18
© Picturepoint: p. 25

THE WINE CHRONICLES

RUNNING PRESS
PHILADELPHIA · LONDON

for Susan

ACKNOWLEDGMENTS

I am deeply indebted to my friend Georges Perrier, who gave me a wine cellar; and to Jim Weinrott and Frank Splan, who helped me figure out how to fill it. We all grew up together in the *métier*.

I am also forever grateful to Janine Mermet, who welcomed me into my adopted culture, despite the obvious fact that there was nothing in my background to recommend me; and to Robert Ampeau, who is one of the greatest wine makers in the world. Many years ago he gave me what is now a dog-eared copy of Max Leglise's *Une Initiation à la Dégustation des Grands Vins*.

My brother Dave contributed most of the good ideas here, and my brother Pete corrected my awkward English. Our colleagues at Moore Brothers, including Dale Belville, Joe DiLuzio, Brian Healy, Chris Kirlakovsky, Jonathan Krieger, John Masino, Kevin McCann, Dave McDuff, Jonathan Read, Megan Shawver, Kathryn Shockor, and Eric Tuverson all made important contributions to the content, but I alone am responsible for omissions and inaccuracies.

Of course, it goes without saying that the world would be a smaller, bleaker place, and this little book would never have existed, were it not for the extraordinary (and often thankless) contribution of the wine growers of the world. They are the courageous, devoted stewards of a heritage that belongs to all of us.

INTRODUCTION

W e'll never know when and where wine was first made, but one thing we can be sure of is that nobody invented it. Wine was an accidental discovery, inevitable wherever grapes were gathered and stored in waterproof containers. Whenever and wherever wine was discovered, it was never forgotten. The record of literature, from the story of Noah to *Wine Spectator*, confirms its special status in Western culture.

Yet drinking wine isn't natural to most of us. We didn't grow up in homes where wine was on the table every day; where even as small children we were permitted a little glass with meals. We find its many attractions compelling, and hear from medical experts how good it is for us, but wine drinking is a foreign practice—weighed down by a heavy load of psychological and social implications that make its natural adoption an awkward process.

There are the self-aggrandizing experts who make it all unnecessarily difficult, promoting their "fine-wine lifestyle," replete with formality and ceremony, where the acquisition of expertise (and 100 point wines) is almost a competitive sport. They bandy about silly insider jargon (like "ZH quality!"), which is as meaningless as it is pretentious, and which discourages the interest of normal, thoughtful people.

The endless variety of wine itself, which is fascinating, can also be intimidating, making the "just drink what you like" advice of self-appointed wine educators the easiest for novices to embrace, even if it eventually frustrates people who want to learn more. Just drinking what you like sounds great, but unless you cultivate a fearless, cheerful willingness to taste more kinds of wines, and taste them with an open mind (especially the ones about which you know absolutely nothing), you won't learn anything.

If you're like many whose curiosity about wine has sometimes been discouraged by these, and other obstacles, please don't give up. This little compendium of common sense (which isn't the same thing as common *wisdom*) is meant to be helpful, though not comprehensive. Plenty of excellent sources with much more detailed information are widely available. This is a book for people who want to teach *themselves* about wine. Most of it will be written by you, on the pages that follow this brief introduction to wine. By writing it, you will begin to teach yourself how to judge the real, intrinsic quality of the wines you taste, regardless of whether or not you actually "like" every single one of them. You will learn how to select better wines, however much or however little you pay for them. The accumulated notes on the wines you taste will become a valuable resource as an aid to your memory, and the process of writing them will exercise your powers of observation and help you to cultivate the habit of careful tasting. If you find in the end that you enjoy wine more, then this introduction to the book you've written will have been a success.

WHICH WINE?

Your tasting notes will be meaningful only if they are attached to clearly identified wines, which means that one of the first things you need to know is how to read the labels. Labels not only identify every wine as a unique product; they also answer important questions about the contributing factors that determine how it tastes. The four most critical, in order of importance, are:

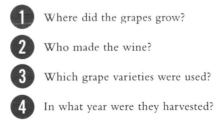

1. Where did the grapes grow?
2. Who made the wine?
3. Which grape varieties were used?
4. In what year were they harvested?

You probably already feel confident about your ability to read the labels on wine from the New World, which includes the United States, Australia, New Zealand, South America and South Africa.

California alone is the source of 90 percent of the wine drunk in America, so they are the labels you're most likely to see. New World labels always identify a brand, and most of them specify a grape variety, so "Laurel Glen Cabernet Sauvignon" and "Talley Chardonnay" are probably meaningful concepts to you even if you've never tasted the wines. We should establish here that Cabernet Sauvignon and Chardonnay aren't *kinds* of wine. They're the names of grape varieties, and nothing more.

You're not alone, either, if you're less comfortable with European wine labels, which usually make no mention of grape varieties. Experience in the Old World has consistently demonstrated that the origin of the grapes is critically important to how the wines made from them taste, so the name of a place is usually the most prominent feature on those labels. Places that are sources of distinctive wines are sometimes called *appellations*. Within each country, a government bureau supervises the production of wine, regulating such issues as the boundaries of the appellations, the winemaking practices, the permitted or required grape varieties, and the permitted maximum yields.

Here's an example of how two different French wines are labeled: The first wine is made by Jean-Marie Raveneau, a fine producer of distinctive white wines from vineyards near the town of Chablis in the Burgundy region of France. Good wines from Chablis are pale green, steely, and high in natural acidity. They are nothing at all like the second wine, made by Dominique Lafon, who is an excellent producer in another part of Burgundy. Lafon's vines grow near the village of Meursault, and give wine that is golden, honeyed, and higher in alcohol, but lower in acidity, than Raveneau's. Both are made from Chardonnay grapes.

If these wines were labeled like New World wines, we'd see "Raveneau Chardonnay" and "Lafon Chardonnay" side by side in liquor stores and on restaurant wine lists, but we'd have no idea what they taste like. Nothing on the labels would indicate how dramatically different they are, or that neither one tastes remotely like California Chardonnay. Happily, in the real world one is labeled Chablis, and the other Meursault. In this example, the European labels that name the wines for their places of origin are even more informative than California labels, despite the absence of the word "Chardonnay."

The problem with the European labels is that they assume our knowledge of the winemaking practices and grape varieties associated with each place name. And, they sometimes create de facto brands out of the appellations, which can lead to more confusion. Some appellations, such as Champagne, are overvalued because of culturally conditioned prestige, which the best wines may deserve, but most ordinary Champagnes definitely do not. Others, like Chablis, are debased for no reason other than the casual misuse of language in English-speaking countries, where jug-wine producers appropriated the name. When I was a sommelier I heard this response more often than not if I recommended one of Raveneau's beautiful wines: "Oh, I want something better than Chablis! Can't you recommend a good Chardonnay?" The problem with New World wine labels is that they, too, have the effect of creating de facto brands—but out of the grape varieties. For many Americans, Chardonnay means "white wine."

In the end, every label should answer the same four critical questions we need to ask if we are to infer how the wine will taste, and we should be able to decipher it. The difference between New and Old World labels is only in how they present the same information.

WHAT MATTERS?

THE PLACE

One of the most important questions you can ask about any wine is this: what *place* is it from? The answer will tell you about the actual content of the wine. No agricultural product can convey a more accurate sense of the place from which it comes than wine. Grapes are the medium, and winemakers are the artists, but the place exists before the wine. Producers in the Old World accept this as self-evident.

European and California wines, for example, taste different, even when they're made from the same grape varieties. Climate plays an important role, though perhaps not exactly in the way you might expect. Napa is at the latitude of Algiers, and the vineyards of Burgundy are at the latitude of Québec, but July temperatures in Carneros, California and Beaune, France aren't all that different. Europe is warmed by the Gulf Stream, and California is cooled by the Pacific Ocean, canceling out expected temperature differences related to latitude. What makes the grapes different is the light, which is brighter in California. The result is a shorter growing season, earlier ripening grapes, and California wines that are generally sweeter and more alcoholic than European wines. August harvests, which are unusual in France, are normal in California.

A thousand years of experience in Europe has shown that two wines made from the same grape variety, but grown in separate vineyards, can be strikingly different, even when the vineyards border one another. It almost seems as if some vineyard boundaries were drawn where the wine began to

taste different, rather than where there was a convenient, notable topographic feature like a grove of trees or a stream. In Burgundy's Côte d'Or, and on the Mosel in Germany, for example, wines like those from the Clos des Lambrays and the Wehlener Sonnenuhr seem not only to describe, but actually to

identify the places they come from. The idea is expressed in the Burgundian concept of *climat,* which encapsulates every variable of climate, topography, soil, and ecology that contributes to the uniqueness of a place and has an effect on its wine.

In addition to the variables of physical environment associated with each place, the culture of the people who live there also plays a determining role in the characteristics of its wines. European wine culture is rooted in agricultural communities, where wine was originally just another important source of calories, produced by farmers on land where nothing but vines would grow. In these areas, wine is a daily habit, but is rarely drunk without food, so each wine was developed to give it characteristics that made it a natural companion to the local cuisine.

Madiran and Cahors, for example, which come from the rural southwest of France, are tannic, intensely flavored, dry red wines that are delicious to drink alongside the meat and beans cooked in duck fat that features prominently in Gascon cuisine. However, some people find them unacceptably astringent without food. In contrast, many red wines from Provence and the southern Rhône are supple and fruity. They evolved in the company of a much more varied cuisine that features mussels, langoustines, and red mullet from the Mediterranean, as well as lamb, olive oil, and herbs from the hills. Cuisine Provençale is even international; it's influenced by the Spaniards, Moroccans, Italians, and French, who all live there together. So Provençal wine needs to be more versatile than Madiran.

This factor may be a good one for us to remember when we order wine in restaurants. If we want red wine that will accommodate a variety of menu choices, we might do well to avoid the ubiquitous California Cabernet Sauvignon and red Bordeaux that dominate so many wine lists. Like Chianti Riserva, Brunello di Montalcino, and Barolo, their most obvious structural characteristic, tannin, is common in wines that evolved to accompany meat. They're fine with roast beef and lamb, but they don't do much for grilled chicken or red-sauced pasta, to say nothing of roasted halibut or lobster.

Wine culture in the New World bypassed any attachment to local cuisines. Though wine has been made in California since the eighteenth century, the roots of modern New World wine culture are in the 1950s, when wine drinking was gradually adopted by the generation returning from the war in Europe.

In the beginning, the new California wines found acceptance only by imitating certain French wines that British aristocrats had already established as international classics. The fascination of the English with claret (red Bordeaux) and port, and their original practice of drinking different wines from different places at the same meal underpinned international wine culture and its aesthetic values. Though not a wine-producing country, England exerted profound early influence on modern wine styles. Like the English language they spoke, the wines the British drank, including Bordeaux, Burgundy, and Champagne from France, Rieslings from the Mosel and Rhine in Germany, and fortified wine from Portugal, became familiar throughout the world. And these wines served as models for the wines produced in all of Britain's former colonies.

It's no accident that Chardonnay and Cabernet Sauvignon became the dominant varieties in California. At the time, white Burgundies (which are made from Chardonnay grapes) and red Bordeaux (which are made with Cabernet Sauvignon grapes) were the two most prestigious wine types in the world.

In 1976 *Time* magazine reported that two Napa wines, a Château Montelena Chardonnay and a

Stag's Leap Wine Cellars Cabernet Sauvignon, had outscored their aristocratic French competition at a blind tasting staged by an English wine merchant. Remarkably, the tasting took place in Paris and was judged by important French connoisseurs. Interest in California Chardonnay and Cabernet Sauvignon surged, and a new, uniquely American set of aesthetic standards for wine was established.

Wines that the Europeans thought "elegant" were deemed "thin," and the sweet vanilla flavor of new oak barrels came to be seen as an indication of high quality. Any reference that the wine itself made to a particular geographic origin (which would have been expected of meaningful wine in Europe) was often obscured in California by heavy-handed winemaking. It became irrelevant, anyway, compared with the requirement that the wine be big, dramatic, and smooth. Today, one more consequence of globalization is that these are the dominant values in international wine, resulting in Ribera del Duero that tastes like Silver Oak Cabernet Sauvignon, and Saint-Véran that tastes like Beringer Chardonnay.

Notwithstanding the proliferation of generic, international wine, fine distinctions of place based on topography and microclimate *do* apply in the New World. Every year, the Bureau of Alcohol, Tobacco, and Firearms approves new American Viticultural Areas (AVAs), which are America's answer to European appellations. In Australia, the government regulates place names through the Label Integrity Programme (LIP), with the same effect. Though no specific grape varieties are required for the use of an AVA or an Australian "Geographical Indication," they amount to official recognition that obvious, consistent differences exist among wines that come from different places. Pinot Noir from the Russian River in Sonoma tastes different than Pinot Noir from Willamette in Oregon, for example. In Australia, Cabernet Sauvignon from Margaret River in the west tastes different than Cabernet Sauvignon from McLaren Vale in the south.

Though the number of place names appearing on wine labels is growing and may be overwhelming, there is a helpful general rule that can be applied in both the Old and the New Worlds: Wines with labels that precisely locate their origins are usually more meaningful than wines with vague, general appellations. Chardonnay from the Arroyo Grande AVA is certain to be more distinctive than Chardonnay labeled "Coastal" or "California." The same is true of Cabernet Sauvignon from Coonawarra, compared with Cabernet Sauvignon labeled "South Australia."

THE HUMAN CONTENT

The intrinsic quality of every wine resides in the intrinsic quality of the grapes that it is made from—quality that can be guaranteed only by the name of the producer on the label. Learning how to read the labels for information they are required to provide about the producer's role in making the wine is the most valuable skill you can acquire. It won't guarantee that you will like every wine you decide to buy, but it can help you avoid wasting your time and money on bottles that are unlikely to teach you anything about wine.

There are essentially two kinds of producers: those who grow their own grapes and make their own wines, and those who buy wine in bulk, which they market under their own labels. Which kind

THE HUMAN CONTENT
(Mick Unti is a fine small producer in Healdsburg in Sonoma County, CA.)

UNTI

THE PLACE
(Dry Creek Valley is an AVA that is a source of distinctive red wines.)

DRY CREEK VALLEY

THE GRAPES
(If the wine is made of at least 75% of a single variety, it may be labeled as that variety.)

ZINFANDEL

THE VINTAGE

1999

84% ZINFANDEL 10% SYRAH
3% PETITE SIRAH 3% SANGIOVESE

THE GRAPESS
(Here the blend is fully described.)

THE HUMAN CONTENT
(Unti grew all of the grapes used in this wine.)

GROWN, PRODUCED AND BOTTLED
BY UNTI VINEYARDS HEALDSBURG CA

ALCOHOL 14.1% BY VOLUME

of producer made any particular wine is indicated on the label. Whether it's proudly spelled out or obscured in ambiguous phrases, every label provides an indication of the concentration of the wine's human content.

In California, a winery that ferments a minimum of 75 percent of the juice that goes into a wine may use the phrase "Produced and Bottled" on its label. If 100 percent of the grapes are grown in a vineyard owned or controlled by the winery, the bottle may be labeled with the phrase "Grown, Produced, and Bottled" at the winery. If the grapes come exclusively from the winery's own vineyards, and both the vineyards and the winery are located in the viticultural area (AVA) named on the label, the winery may use the phrase "Estate Bottled." These are all meaningful, and you should look for these phrases on the labels. On the other hand, "Made and Bottled" is an intentionally misleading phrase. It indicates only that a minimum of 10 percent of the wine was actually fermented at the location where it was bottled. And most wines labeled with such pretentious phrases as "Cellared and Bottled," or "Vinted and Bottled" are as meaningless as the labels themselves. The human content in such wines is diluted, and few of them are likely to contribute to your wine education.

The same kind of information about the producers is required on European wine labels. An Italian grower is a *viticoltore*, who may produce estate-bottled wine at his *azienda agricola* that is labeled "Imbottigliato all'Origine." Sometimes the information is given in English, too, as "Estate Bottled." On the other hand, a company that buys in bulk or vinifies purchased grapes is an *azienda vinicola*. A co-operative winery, where growers who don't make their own wine take their grapes to be vinified, is a *cantina sociale*, which is sometimes named for the *produttori* (plural) of the area who are members.

THE PLACE
(Guarantees the place of origin, and establishes quality standards.)

THE HUMAN CONTENT
(Indicates the wine was bottled at the same place the grapes were grown, by a *viticoltore*, a producer who grows his own grapes.)

THE PLACE
(Germano's address)

THE PLACE
(Barolo is a village in Italy.)

THE VINTAGE

THE PLACE
(Cerretta is a single vineyard in the village of Barolo.)

THE HUMAN CONTENT
(Germano Ettore is a *viticoltore* based in Barolo.)

THE PLACE
(Gevrey-Chambertin is a village in the Côte d'Or in Burgundy.)

THE VINTAGE
(*Millésime* means "vintage" in French.)

THE HUMAN CONTENT
(Rion purchased some of the grapes, acting as a négociant, which is confirmed by this phrase.)

GEVREY-CHAMBERTIN
APPELLATION GEVREY-CHAMBERTIN CONTRÔLÉE

MILLÉSIME
1999
PATRICE RION

13%Alc. Vol
*Mis en bouteilles
dans nos caves*

750 ml
*21700 Prémeaux ·
Produit de France*

THE PLACE
(Guarantees the place of origin.)

THE HUMAN CONTENT
(Patrice Rion is a fine négociant producer.)

THE PLACE
(Rion's address)

French wines bottled by producers identified as *propriétaires, récoltants,* or *viticulteurs* are made by farmers who grow their own grapes. Look for estate-bottled wines that are *mis en bouteilles* (bottled) *à la propriété, au domaine,* or *au château*. Labels with the ambiguous phrase "Mis en Bouteilles dans nos Caves" (bottled in our cellars) identify wines that come from producers called *négociants,* who blend and bottle wine grown by others. Although there are certainly many good wines bottled by the best *négociants,* particularly in Burgundy, the most sought-after wines are almost always bottled by the growers themselves.

THE VINTAGE

THE PLACE
(Bacharach is a small village on the Rhine River. Wolfshöhle is a single steep, black slate vineyard.)

THE "DRYNESS"
(*Halbtrocken* means "half-dry.")

THE HUMAN CONTENT
(*Gutsabfüllung* means "estate-bottled.")

THE PLACE
(Mittelrhein is a small region along the Rhine.)

THE HUMAN CONTENT
(A *weingut* is an estate-bottling winery)

RATZENBERGER

·1991er·
Bacharacher Wolfshöhle
Riesling Spätlese·
·halbtrocken·

Qualitätswein mit Prädikat
A. P. Nr. 1 698 179 04 92

alc. 9,5% vol · Gutsabfüllung   e 75 cl
· MITTELRHEIN

· WEINGUT RATZENBERGER · D-6533 BACHARACH ·

THE HUMAN CONTENT
(Ratzenberger is a small family winery in the Mittelrhein region.)

THE GRAPES
(*Spätlese* means that the Riesling grapes were late harvested.)

THE LEGAL QUALITY
(QmP is the highest quality classification for German wines. QmP wines do not have sugar added to the fermenting juice.)

TASTING APPROVAL NUMBER

THE PLACE
(Ratzenberger's address)

THE "DRYNESS"
(Wines described as *brut* are the driest sparkling wines.)

THE PLACE
(Champagne is a region in north-central France)

THE PLACE
(Michel's address)

THE VINTAGE

THE HUMAN CONTENT
(José Michel and his son run a small family winery in the village of Moussy in the Canton of Epernay in Champagne.)

THE HUMAN CONTENT
(A *recolant manipulant* producer grows all the grapes used in the wines.)

You can even estimate the concentration of the human content of sparkling wines from the Champagne region in France ("real" Champagne), where producers are identified by a two letter code that precedes a license number of six or seven digits. "N.M." *(négociant manipulant)* means that the producer purchases some, if not all, of the grapes used to make the Champagnes he sells. "N.M." producers generally buy grapes from several different sources and blend them together to achieve a consistent house style. All of the famous brands like Moët et Chandon and G.H. Mumm, are *négociant manipulant* producers. The best "N.M." wines are the top *cuvées* like Dom Perignon, which are very expensive. There's a good chance, however, that you'll find equally special Champagne at lower prices that come from "R.M." *(récoltant manipulant)* or "S.R." *(société de récoltant)* producers, who grow 100 percent of the grapes used to make their wines. "R.M." and "S.R." Champagnes may be more expressive of a special place of origin as well.

Think of Champagne this way: If it's a famous brand, it's made in large quantities and may not be as interesting as a brand you've never heard of. Check carefully to see if the label indicates an "R.M." or "S.R." producer. Or, if you think the retailer or the waiter will know what you're talking about, just ask for a "grower's Champagne." It may be a revelation, especially if you think you don't like Champagne.

Simply put, wine is like any other produce. If you'd never tasted a fat, lumpy beefsteak tomato that came from a farm stand in July, you'd probably be perfectly satisfied with (if not excited by) the bland pink billiard balls that pass for tomatoes in supermarkets in February. But if you have enough experience to know the difference, you're probably a good judge of tomato quality. You can become a good judge of wine quality, too—by having more experiences with meaningful wines, which are always made from good grapes, grown in good places, by good farmers. You won't find them among the products of giant agribusiness corporations.

THE GRAPES

Vitis vinifera, the wine bearing vine, is the only species that gives grapes suitable for the production of fine wine. Ampelographers who study and describe it believe that vinifera originated in Asia, in the area beyond the Black Sea. The accidental discovery of wine made the vines an important crop that quickly spread throughout the Mediterranean and Europe. The Phoenicians and Greeks, and later the Romans, all planted grapes wherever they would ripen.

Today there are over ten thousand varieties of vinifera in cultivation, including about one thousand that are used to make wine. Most of them have little significance, but a few dozen are responsible for most of the wines you will ever taste. A few among them, like Pinot Noir and Riesling, are sometimes called "noble" varieties. They regularly give distinctive wines that are expressive of their vineyard origins, and that, over time in a good cellar, develop aromatics and flavors that can't be imitated by any means other than bottle age.

Here is a personal catalog of wine grapes with descriptions, listed in no particular order of importance (and which is by no means comprehensive):

RED WINE GRAPES

PINOT NOIR is the grape responsible for the red wines of Burgundy (which include some of the greatest wines in the world), and is a component of most of the sparkling wines of Champagne. It is an ancient variety, indisputably one of the noblest, and may have been directly selected from among the wild vines of continental France as long as two thousand years ago (ampelographers, who use DNA to classify varieties, are unable to identify any known progenitor of Pinot Noir). The name refers to the tight, pinecone-shaped clusters of small, black, thin-skinned grapes.

Wines made from these grapes are less tannic than Cabernet Sauvignon wines, so they are usually more accessible in their youth, and evolve more quickly. When young, they smell of red fruits rather than black, often with a little clove. The best, however, can be long-lived wines that develop complex aromatics, including the smell of mushrooms, damp forest floor, and even strawberry preserves. In addition to the wines of Burgundy and Champagne, there are successful Pinot Noir wines in Oregon and New Zealand, though in general it hasn't traveled as successfully as some other varieties.

CABERNET SAUVIGNON is the most widely traveled black grape in the world. It came to prominence in the late eighteenth century, when the "Great Estates" of Bordeaux were established, and a taste for bottle-aged wine was growing in the British market (bottles and corks, which made ageworthy wine possible, had only just become widely available). Today, Cabernet Sauvignon is the most important component in the wines of the Médoc; and as a varietal wine, is responsible for the best red wines of California, Washington State, Australia, New Zealand, and South Africa.

Distinguishing features of the grapes include small berry size, a high seed-to-pulp ratio, and a thick, blue-black skin. The wines are often described as smelling like blackcurrant, with eucalyptus and mint evident in some of the New World versions, and leaves and cut grass in cooler climate wines. The flavors marry well with oak, so most fine Cabernet Sauvignon wines are aged in small barrels.

MERLOT is the most widely planted red wine grape in Bordeaux, primarily because it ripens early, meaning healthy grapes can almost always be harvested before the annual arrival of Atlantic rainstorms in the early fall. Merlot is responsible for the great wines of Pomerol, Saint-Emilion, and the other Right Bank appellations. An important component of many other wines in the southwest of France, Merlot is also widely grown in Friuli, the Veneto, and Trentino-Alto Adige in Italy, as well as in the New World, as a varietal wine that is expected to be softer and fruitier than Cabernet Sauvignon.

There are few exceptions, however, to Right Bank Bordeaux and some of the wines from California, that achieve real complexity. Part of Merlot's attraction, undoubtedly, is that the flavors are compatible with the flavors of oak. Popular, cheap Merlots, like popular, cheap Chardonnays, are likely to be juiced up with unfermented grape juice concentrate for body, and pumped over oak chips to simulate barrel aging. Most of them aren't fine wine.

SYRAH is probably better known today by its Australian synonym **SHIRAZ**. The grape is believed to have come to the northern Rhône with Phocaen Greek colonists, who may have brought it from Persia. In the appellations Hermitage, Côte Rôtie, and Cornas, it gives powerful, black pepper and lily scented wines with tremendous capacity for aging. Syrah also finds its way into Southern Rhône and Provence blends, and is produced as a varietal wine in other parts of the Midi. In addition to Australia, where Shiraz gives viscous, alcoholic wines loaded with sweet black fruit, it can be very successful in California and Tuscany.

NEBBIOLO is clearly a noble variety, responsible for some of the greatest wines of Italy, including Barolo and Barbaresco, which grow on the Langhe hills around the town of Alba. Outside of small amounts grown in Valle d'Aosta and Lombardia, Nebbiolo is mostly confined to Piemonte, and is not a successful international traveler. The grapes have very thick skins, which give tannic wines that are intensely and distinctively aromatic of rose petals, truffles, licorice and even road tar.

SANGIOVESE is the noble grape of Italy's center. Chianti, Brunello di Montalcino, and Vino Nobile di Montepulciano are all examples of Sangiovese based wines, which are typically tannic, with marked acidity and a modest garnet red color. Even in ripe vintages, they have astringency, which makes them very suitable accompaniment to the grilled-meat based cuisine of Tuscany. In the D.O.C. Carmignano, Sangiovese is traditionally blended with Cabernet Sauvignon, which adds flesh and color. Today, many producers include Cabernet Sauvignon in their Chianti as well.

ZINFANDEL is California's own noble black grape variety, though its origins are certainly European. It was known as early as the 1830s in Massachusetts, and by 1900 was California's most important red wine variety. The best Zinfandels are moderately tannic, with refreshing acidity and lots of deep black fruit.

White Zinfandel—a pale, rosé-colored beverage, usually slightly sweet—was initially conceived during the white wine boom of the 1970s as a way to commercialize the huge acreage of existing Zinfandel, which had been traditionally vinified as deep red wine. It is, however, strictly a cheap, pop-

commodity, and should not be mistaken for fine wine.

OTHER BLACK GRAPE VARIETIES with more limited geographic distribution can be just as noble as these. No serious list would omit **CABERNET FRANC**, which is blended with Merlot in Bordeaux, and gives distinctive wines in the middle Loire, such as Chinon and Bourgueil. Beaujolais, one of the most undervalued and versatile of French wines, wouldn't exist without **GAMAY NOIR**, nor southern Rhônes and Provence wines without **GRENACHE**. In the southwest of France, **MALBEC** and **TANNAT** are clearly important as components of wines like Cahors and Madiran. And **FER SERVADOU, DURAS**, and **NEGRETTE** all have their place, as well.

In Italy, **BARBERA, DOLCETTO, GRIGNOLINO**, and **FREISA** all contribute to the rich variety of Piemontese wine. **AGLIANICO** is the grape of Taurasi and the wines of Basilicata, and Amarone would not exist without **CORVINA**. Even **GAGLIOPPO**, which came to Italy with the Greeks and is responsible for Cirò, has an ancient and distinguished history. As Cremissa, it was offered to victorious athletes at the ancient Olympics. Today Cirò still fortifies the Italian Olympic team.

In Spain, Rioja and Ribera del Duero are made from **TEMPRANILLO**, and no good Porto could be made without **TOURIGA NACIONAL**.

WHITE WINE GRAPES

RIESLING is the world's greatest white wine grape. That's not just my opinion, it's the opinion of respected authors and connoisseurs such as Michael Broadbent, Hugh Johnson and Jancis Robinson. It was also the opinion of André Julien, Cyrus Redding, George Saintsbury, and Frank Schoonmaker. In fact, before the outbreak of the first World War, Rieslings from Germany were the most expensive white wines in the world.

Today Riesling suffers from an image that was thoroughly debased by the flood of vapid, cheap sugar water that big German merchant houses exported in the 1960s, 1970s, and 1980s—including just about every German wine that casual consumers encountered at the time. For the record, almost no wines labeled Liebfraumilch, Zeller Schwartze Katz, Piesporter Michelsberg, or Niersteiner Gutes Domtal contain even a drop of Riesling.

When planted in a good vineyard, Riesling communicates a sense of place more vividly than any other white variety. No good Mosel Riesling could be mistaken for a Rheingau wine, for example. And whether it's vinified dry, medium, or sweet, Riesling's appetizing acidity makes it a versatile partner to a wide range of food. The best wines come from Germany, Alsace, and Austria, but the grape also travels well, and there are excellent wines in the Finger Lakes District of New York State, the Anderson Valley in California, and the Clare Valley in South Australia.

Riesling has the capacity to develop very complex, multilayered aromatics after some years in the bottle, which can't be achieved by any means other than long aging. (I recently drank a thirty-one year old dry Riesling from a steep, black slate vineyard in the Mittelrhein. It was undoubtedly one of the greatest wines I have ever tasted.)

CHENIN BLANC, like Riesling, is a sadly underappreciated noble variety. In appellations like Vouvray, Montlouis, and Savennières, it gives extremely long-lived dry and off-dry wines, with complex aromatics of apples, clean hay, and minerals. When affected by *Botrytis cinerea* (see Sémillon Blanc), in appellations like Coteaux du Layon and Vouvray, the wines can be powerfully sweet, but are never cloying. Like Riesling, Chenin Blanc retains firm acidity, even when harvested late.

The same acidity makes Chenin Blanc an important variety in hot regions like the Central Valley in California, where, along with Colombard, it is widely grown for the production of jug wine. That, unfortunately, debases its reputation in the varietally conscious New World.

CHARDONNAY is the great blank canvas of white wine grape varieties. Its origins were obscure until recently, when ampelographers using DNA mapping techniques were able to show that it is in fact a cross between Pinot Noir and an ancient white variety called Gouais Blanc.

Chardonnay's appeal to growers lies in the ease of its cultivation and its reliable yields. Winemakers love it for its neutral varietal character, which never gets in the way of stylistic flourishes like malolactic fermentation (which makes the wine taste "buttery") and oak barrel aging. Not only does Chardonnay travel well, it can communicate a clear sense of place in vineyards as distant from its origins in continental France as Hawkes Bay, New Zealand and Santa Barbara, California.

In France, Chardonnay is responsible for the great white wines of Burgundy, from appellations like Puligny-Montrachet and Chablis, and it comprises about a third of the vineyard plantings in Champagne. In the New World, Chardonnay is most successful in cool climate vineyards, where it retains acidity. Good, barrel fermented, full malolactic wines come from AVAs such as Santa Cruz Mountains, Arroyo Grande, Russian River, and Anderson Valley.

Cheap versions from hotter regions, like California's Central Valley and South Australia's Riverland, are often made slightly sweet, which requires that they be acidified (citric or tartaric acid is added to make them drinkable). Most are treated to some form of cheap oak flavoring (usually toasted chips), which badly imitates actual barrel aging. They include some of the most popular Chardonnays in the world (millions of cases are sold), but like white Zinfandel, they shouldn't be confused with fine wine.

SAUVIGNON BLANC gives some of the world's most versatile food wines. Its varietal character is assertive and easily recognizable, with piercing aromatics of freshly cut grass and herbs framed in bright, mouthwatering acidity. The most striking pure varietal wines come from the Loire Valley appellations of Sancerre, Pouilly-Fumé, Quincy, and Ménetou Salon, where the wines are described as steely and flinty; and from cool vineyards in New Zealand's Marlborough and Hawkes Bay districts, where intensity of berry and citric fruit aromatics is a distinguishing feature.

In the southwest of France, Sauvignon Blanc is often blended with Sémillon in both dry and sweet wines. The warmer climate results in wines with lower acidity than the wines of the Loire.

As **FUMÉ BLANC** in California, Sauvignon Blanc is sometimes vinified in oak barrels, and may retain perceptible residual sweetness. There are some high quality exceptions, but Sauvignon Blanc in California is mostly seen as an inexpensive alternative to more fashionable oak-aged Chardonnay.

SÉMILLON adds weight and texture when blended with Sauvignon Blanc, and has the special characteristic that it is subject to attack by *Botrytis cinerea*, a common fungus. When *Botrytis* grows on the skins of fully ripe grapes, they become ineffective barriers to evaporation of the grape's water content. In appellations like Sauternes, Barsac, and Monbazillac, where cool, overcast mornings are followed by sunny, breezy afternoons, *Botrytis*-infected grapes shrivel on the vine, looking like raisins covered with cobwebs. Sugar and extract are concentrated, and they can be made into luscious, sweet wines with tremendous potential for bottle age. As a varietal wine, Sémillon is most distinctive in the Hunter Valley of New South Wales in Australia.

VIOGNIER is the grape of Condrieu and Château Grillet in the northern Rhône. Not long ago, these tiny appellations just south of Lyon were the only places in the world where this distinctively aromatic variety was grown. Today, the cultivation of Viognier has spread to the southern Rhône and the Languedoc in France, as well as to California, Australia and South Africa. Languedoc and New World versions lack the special finesse of the northern Rhône wines, but for some, they make up for it in opulence and aromatic intensity.

PINOT GRIGIO is everyone's favorite "crisp" alternative to broader, heavier Chardonnay. The problem is that most of the wine that goes by the name is frankly undistinguished. Even the northern Italian growers who rely on it for cash flow usually prefer their proprietary blends, or their other varietal wines, like those made from **TOCAI FRIULANI** and **NOSIOLA**.

As **PINOT GRIS**, the grape achieves much more in Alsace, where it takes on more weight and exotic perfume, sometimes suggesting truffles and smoke. Good varietal Pinot Gris is also made in Oregon, from grapes grown in both the Rogue Valley and Willamette Valley AVAs.

OTHER IMPORTANT WHITE WINE VARIETIES include **GEWÜRZTRAMINER**, which is undoubtedly the most easily recognized of them all, strikingly marked with the smell of lychee in Alsace and rose petals and pepper in the Pfalz in Germany. It also gives distinctive, fine wine in Alto Adige in northern Italy, where it originated, and in California's Anderson Valley AVA.

Otherwise, in Italy fine wines are made from **GARGANEGA** in the DOC Soave, and **VERDICCHIO** on the Adriatic coast. **MALVASIA** is important in Tuscany and Lazio, **FIANO** in Campania, and **ARNEIS** and **ERBALUCE** in Piemonte. **CORTESE**, which is the grape of Gavi, is overrated. Spain, Austria, and Hungary round out the short list with **ALBARIÑO**, **GRÜNER VELTLINER**, and **FURMINT**, respectively.

THE VINTAGES

Just as the quality of all produce is subject to the vagaries of weather, wine quality depends in part on weather patterns, which are unique to every year. Excessive heat and drought in the summer can arrest photosynthesis, causing the vines to "shut down," which interrupts the ripening process. Low acidity may result, and the wines may taste "baked." Heavy rain before and during the harvest can result in rotten grapes and diluted wine. In the case of wines like Bordeaux, which are made from a mix of different grape varieties—each of which flowers at a slightly different time—unseasonable cold and rain in late spring can limit the size of one or more of the crops, influencing the final mix of grapes in the wine.

But shopping for wine on the basis of vintage alone is a mistake that eventually will lead to disappointment. There are plenty of terrible 1997 Italian wines, made or assembled by incompetent producers who failed to manage their yields, or by greedy opportunists who simply engaged in fraud, knowing that anything with 1997 on the label would sell because the year had already been declared a "Vintage of the Century."

Good wine should almost make itself when conditions result in plenty of healthy, ripe fruit. The pleasant surprises sometimes come in the "off" vintages, when the best producers distinguish themselves from the rest. They make less wine when conditions are difficult, but they make outstanding wine regularly, because they rigorously select only the best grapes. It's expensive for them to do the extra work, and they have to charge less for the wine because journalists have already panned the vintage. But this means they can be excellent values.

The real, practical value of the vintage date on most wine labels is that it tells us the age of the wine, which can be an indication of its freshness. Most of the appeal of wines like Beaujolais and northern Italian Pinot Grigios lies in their immediate fruitiness, which fades in time. They should be purchased and drunk as young as possible. Even wine with the capacity to develop complexity with age, like fine California Cabernet Sauvignon and Burgundy, should be purchased young. Getting it out of the distribution system and into good storage as soon as possible may minimize damage caused by poor conditions. Old wine of unknown provenance isn't worth buying.

HOW FRESH IS IT?

If you ever wondered why that great eight dollar Montepulciano you had last summer in Perugia tasted so much better than the Italian wine you drink when you're home in the U.S., you're not alone. Many travelers notice how much better wine tastes when it's drunk at the source, even if they don't know why. The answer is really quite simple (and has nothing to do with added sulfites): the wine you drank in Italy was fresh, whereas much of the wine you drink in the U.S. is stale, damaged by heat in transportation and storage. It's one of the dirty little secrets of the wine distribution system. Every single link in the chain of events that gets wine from the sources of production to its markets is fraught with peril. But many importers, distributors, and retailers of wine don't believe that customers are able to recognize heat damaged wine, so few take the precautions necessary to protect it.

Refrigerated trucks that are used routinely to transport all kinds of produce are rarely used for wine. Temperature-controlled shipping containers that are available to importers add little to the cost of transportation, yet very few use them. And almost all wine languishes for a time in hot liquor warehouses and warm retail stores and restaurants. The result is that most wine bears little resemblance to the wine that left the producers' cellars.

Here's a wine-buying tip: Carefully inspect every bottle before you buy it. If it's young wine, be sure that the level is within a half-inch or so of the cork. Look for obvious signs of leakage, such as dried rivulets of wine originating under the foil capsule that covers the top of the bottle, and stains on the label. Try to twist the foil capsule; it should spin freely (of course there are exceptions, like shrink fitted plastic and wax capsules that won't spin even when the bottle is perfectly fresh). Otherwise, if it doesn't spin, it's likely that the capsule is glued tight by wine that was forced past the cork because of heat, resulting in the goopy, caramel-smelling substance you've probably encountered under a capsule at one time or another.

Also pay attention to the temperature. Feel the bottle. If it's warm, it's not likely to be in good condition. Remember that wine is like milk; it's an agricultural product. You want to drink it fresh. There is nothing in the so-called "etiquette" of wine that should prevent you from doing the same when you buy it in a restaurant.

TASTING

J ust the idea of good wine tasting technique sounds pretentious, and its actual practice looks silly and sounds disgusting to most normal people. Students in my wine classes laugh when I demonstrate it—especially the spitting, which is necessary whenever more than a few wines are being tasted. When they first see it, I'm sure they think it's nothing more than a series of affectations I've adopted in the hope of drawing attention to my expertise. Actually, it's a sequence of component parts of the method by which I thoroughly and efficiently examine a wine using all of my senses. Virtually everyone has the physical ability to become a good taster. We all have a tongue and a nose. We only need to learn how to use them efficiently.

Our tongues, we recall from high school biology, are chemically sensitive to saltiness, sweetness, tartness, and bitterness. Sweetness and tartness are measures of sugar and acidity, which are important components of wine. Our tongues are also exquisitely sensitive to texture, which can help us measure how much tannin and extract there is in the wine we taste. *Tannins* are complex phenolic compounds found in many plant parts that have the effect of astringency in our mouths, and *extract* is essentially everything in wine that isn't volatile. The rest of the lining of our mouths is also sensitive to alcohol, which is perceived as warmth and weight. Extract and alcohol combine to give us the impression of *body* in wine.

But it's how well we use our noses that determines how well we taste. We need to recognize that we actually smell most of what we think we are tasting. When we chew on a piece of lamb, for exam-

ple, we know it's lamb, not because of a unique combination of saltiness, sweetness, tartness, and bitterness measured by our tongues, but because the bellows motion of chewing it pumps warm air containing lamb molecules past the most sensitive olfactory receptors we have, which are located behind our soft palates. These receptors are primarily stimulated via the *retronasal passage*, which connects our mouths with our noses. The flavor of the lamb is actually an amalgam of its smell, via these receptors, and the simpler chemical and physical impressions it leaves in our mouths.

The first requirement for the practice of good wine tasting technique is a good glass. One of the best is called the ISO glass, named for the International Standards Organization. The ISO recognizes that the shape and dimension of a glass influence how wine tastes, and it recommends a standard glass to ensure that a single wine tastes the same to different tasters, no matter where they are.

However, there are many other glasses that work just as well. I prefer to use the "Gourmet" tasting glass, part of a series called Vinum that is made by the Austrian crystal producer Riedel. This glass is inexpensive and durable, with a short stem, so it fits nicely in the top rack of the dishwasher. The main characteristics of a good glass are that it is of sufficient capacity to hold enough wine without being filled more than a quarter of the way, and that it curves inward toward the opening.

Once the glass is selected and the wine is poured, examine it carefully, in natural or incandescent light. (Fluorescent light washes out the color of white wines and distorts the color of reds, making young wine appear blue and older wine appear brown). Look through the wine at a white background if it helps. Swirl the glass so that the wine coats the inside, and notice how it slides back down the glass surface, forming what are sometimes called *legs* or *tears*. Then forget about them. Contrary to silly common lore about *glycerine* and *viscosity*, the legs of wine have *no* significance whatsoever, except as an unreliable indicator of alcoholic strength.

Swirl the glass anyway, or hold it at a diagonal and rotate it, so that the entire inside surface is coated with wine. Put your nose in the glass, as far as it will fit, and inhale

slowly and deeply. Then sniff forcefully two or three times. Bring the glass to your lips and take in a good measure of the wine; at least enough that you can get it to every surface inside your mouth, including between your lips and teeth and as far back as possible. Tip your head forward a little, so that the wine in your mouth pools against your lips, and draw in a little air, as if you were whistling in reverse. Then chew, paying special attention to the flavor impressions you get from smelling the wine via your retronasal passage. Swallow or spit, and follow with two or three more quick inhalations through your open mouth. Don't be self-conscious about how it looks or sounds, and don't be shy about spitting. Good tasters develop good aim, and practice will make it all seem natural.

Aside from its practical value whenever critical evaluation of wine is part of the agenda, understanding the component parts of good wine tasting technique will lead you to habits that may make wine drinking more rewarding. Here is one of the most worthwhile, practical wine-drinking tips you will read here: Drink wine out of good glasses. That doesn't mean expensive crystal, or for that matter, ISO or Riedel Vinum "Gourmet" glasses.

What makes a good glass is its shape, not its price. It's a matter of chemistry, aerodynamics, and physiology. Good glasses have sides that curve inward towards the opening. They contain and protect the volume of air above the surface of the wine, where aromas accumulate, and keep it in the glass, even when the glass is moved. Straight-sided, flared glasses actually encourage turbulence, which forcefully pulls aromatics away from the surface and out of the glass every time it's moved. The wine in those glasses actually tastes watered down, compared with the same wine in a good glass.

Good glasses can only serve their purpose when they contain and protect a sufficient volume of air above the surface of the wine. So the following is just as important a practical wine-drinking tip: Don't overfill the glasses. This seems to be one of the most difficult bad habits for novice wine drinkers to break. At least half of the pleasure in a glass of good wine comes from the aromatics that accumulate in the glass above the wine's surface. So when you pour, leave plenty of room in the glass for your nose. Never fill wineglasses more than a third of the way. Pour wine the way you eat bread at dinner, breaking off a little at a time. Filling the glasses to the top for the sake of economy of effort is like slathering a whole baguette with a stick of butter and eating it like a hoagie. Just the fact that it requires a little more time will have you paying more attention to the wine.

WINE WITH FOOD

O ne of the students who came regularly to my earliest wine classes was a young MBA candidate from Japan. He delighted in telling me about his father—a deep-pocketed investment banker in Kyoto—and the outrageously expensive wines he drank every day. Favorites included Penfold's Grange Hermitage 1971, Heitz Martha's Vineyard Cabernet Sauvignon 1974, and Château Pétrus 1982. He drank them with his *zarusoba* and *sashimi*.

At the risk of contradicting the populist notion, "just drink the wine you like with the food you like," I think it's safe to say that my student's father must have been discovering some pretty bizarre wine and food pairings. But drinking wine with food isn't a natural feature of Japanese culture, and his only desire was to drink the very best wines he knew of, which he did. He could afford it.

So could a certain contingent of power-diners at Le Bec-Fin, in Philadelphia, where I was the sommelier for almost twenty years. Stratospheric prices didn't discourage them from ordering 98 point "Wine of the Year" Marcassin Chardonnays or toasty Maison Verget Corton Charlemagnes to go with their *turbotin au beurre blanc*. It would have been unkind of me to suggest that either of these fabulous $250 wines—paired with a dish as refined and delicate as the baby turbot—was as bizarre a selection as the Japanese businessman's Château Pétrus with sushi. It would have been imprudent, too, to tell them I had a $12 wine in mind that would be a better choice (I was part of the restaurant's overhead). They wouldn't have believed me, anyway.

A good strategy for sommeliers comes from knowing that most recipes in classical cuisine weren't developed in experimental kitchens by chefs who conjured them out of thin air. Like composers and novelists, great chefs are artists who draw inspiration from tradition, which they interpret and refine. In fact, almost every classic dish has an antecedent in some agricultural community's cuisine. Georges Perrier's *lentilles du Puy aux truffes noires*, for example, is really nothing but a refined version of a peasant dish that is traditional in the Roergue in the southwest of France. They have wine, too, in the Roergue: Marcillac, which is excellent with lentils cooked in duck fat.

This example brings us back to the *turbotin au beurre blanc*. The dish originated in the *pays*

Nantais—the country surrounding the port city of Nantes, where the Loire flows into the Bay of Biscay. Fresh, simple seafood is a staple of the local cuisine, and the *beurre blanc* originated there. The wine of the region is Muscadet, which is straightforward, crisp, dry white wine made from a grape called Melon de Bourgogne. When I first tasted the *turbotin* with a five year-old bottle of Léon Boullaut's Muscadet "Grande Garde" it was an electrifying experience. The wine cost about $12.

But successful wine and food pairing isn't some arcane craft that requires years of study to master. The fact is, most wines with sufficient acidity and not too much alcohol or tannin happily accompany most foods. Versatile white wines include un-oaked Sauvignon Blancs, dry and off-dry Rieslings from Germany, and Chenin Blancs from the Loire Valley in France. Red wines that can be served with almost everything include southern Rhône and Provence wines, Cabernet Franc wines from the middle Loire, Beaujolais, Valpolicella, and unoaked Barbera from Piemonte. Barrel-aged Cabernets and Chardonnays are really only at their best with a narrow range of foods, like red meat and rich cream sauces.

The simplest, all-purpose advice is this: Break every rule you like, but drink wine with food as often as possible. Make a note of the most successful (and unsuccessful) pairings you encounter. If you're not afraid of *sashimi* or *bagna caôda*, you shouldn't be afraid of Mosel Riesling or Piemontese Dolcetto, either. Think of how much more exciting cooking and dining are today, now that we're no longer disgusted by the thought of eating raw fish, and Italian cooking means more than spaghetti and meatballs.

HOW MUCH SHOULD YOU PAY?

T he questions I'm asked time after time in wine classes convince me that common wine lore is rife with cherished beliefs that are rooted in misinformation. These myths are repeated over and over so many times that they take on a life of their own, and begin to sound perfectly reasonable.

Nothing in the "fine-wine lifestyle" culture contradicts one of the least helpful of these myths: that the more you pay for wine, the better it will be. The journalists treat wine like a competitive sport, and lavish extravagant praise in the form of the highest scores on wines few people ever actually drink. Such wines are impossible to find and very expensive, but they're definitely aesthetically homogeneous. Almost every one is a big buttery Chardonnay, a dramatic oaky Cabernet, or a toasty chocolaty Merlot. Of course consumers get the message that bigger is better.

To be fair, large-scaled wines like Marcassin Chardonnay and Caymus Special Selection Cabernet Sauvignon can be very impressive. But they're not better wine than Navarro Riesling, simply because their flavors are more dramatic, or their textures more sumptuous—any more than Rubens' *Prometheus Bound* is a better painting than da Vinci's *Mona Lisa* because it's physically bigger.

What all the ballyhoo about full-bodied wine leads to is ten dollar "Chardonnays" and "Merlots" that are nothing but poor imitations of wines consumers think they should aspire to drink. The most popular (read: cheapest) and worst are caricatures of wine—little more than thinly disguised *coolers*, with artificial oak in the place of artificial strawberry (you'll find lots of "vinted" and "cellared" wines in this group). The multi-million case depletions of these products leave little room on restaurant wine lists and liquor store shelves for *real* fine wine that happens to be inexpensive. Observant consumers then learn that the more they pay for their wine, the more likely it will actually be an agricultural product, and the better it will taste.

The truth is, that for about ten dollars a bottle, you *can* actually buy a wide variety of handmade, estate-bottled, small-farm wines. However, they're unlikely to be California wines, and they won't have the words "Chardonnay" or "Merlot" on the labels. The best ten dollar red wines come from the south of France. Look for appellations like Cabardès, Gaillac, Marcillac, and Côtes du Rhône. Be sure they are estate-bottled wines, and avoid "fightin' varietals" like Vin de Pays d'Oc Merlots and Chardonnays. In Italy, really good ten dollar red wine is harder to find, but un-oaked Barbera from Piemonte, and some of the wines of the Veneto and the Marche, such as Valpolicella Classico and Rosso Piceno, can qualify.

Good ten dollar white wines are also likely to be French, from appellations as varied as Alsace, Montravel, and Savoie. But there are also Italian white wines, like some Verdicchios and Soaves from good estate-bottlers, that can be as inexpensive.

In any case, the important thing isn't how much you pay for wine, but how much you care about it. You'll have a wider variety of experiences, and learn a whole lot more about wine, if you open an affordable bottle of meaningful wine every day than you will if you abstain all week and drink a famous Bordeaux in a restaurant on Saturday night.

WRITING YOUR NOTES

There are two obstacles you'll face in your note taking: The first is that an almost irresistible urge to decide that you like or dislike the wine will intrude on your judgment, before you've had sufficient time to assess all of the wine's qualities. The second is that there is no such thing as a universally accepted wine tasting vocabulary.

The glossary at the end of this book defines a few common associative taste descriptors that are in wide use, such as *cedar* and *eucalyptus*, but no lexicon of tasting terms can ever be comprehensive. There are simply too many smells and flavors to be named, and language is inadequate to the task (just try to describe the smell of a pear, without ever using the word *pear*). There is, however, agreement on the definition of the technical terms that describe analytically measurable components of wine, such as *tannin, acidity,* and *extract.* You should learn their meaning, and use them correctly. Consult the glossary for definitions of unfamiliar labeling phrases and the appendices to help you answer the four questions that uniquely identify the wine.

Choose one of the two formats outlined in the following section. The Detailed Journal Entries should be used for recording tasting notes that will be more meaningful to you if they're accompanied by detailed comments, for example, on the condition of the bottle, the food that was served, and the company that was present. These detailed entries may even include the label, which is usually easy to remove by soaking the bottle in hot water. A neater method uses transparent super-adhesive sheets that are available wherever wine accessories are sold. Whichever format you use, follow the tasting procedure described on p. 26. Try to ignore the "I like it" or "I don't like it" conclusion you'll be tempted to reach until *after* you've swallowed or spit out the wine, and considered the length and quality of its finish. Remember that you are trying to teach yourself how to *judge* the quality of the wine, as well as recording your *opinion* of it.

That's why a systematic process is more important than the vocabulary you use. Besides, some notes will sound silly no matter what vocabulary you use. I'm embarrassed to admit that I once wrote the following sentence in an article about German wine: "Contrasting with the baroque, assertive wines of Schmitt-Wagner, Martin Kerpen's Mosel Rieslings are sleek and elegant; more charming than authoritative, yet in no way diffident or self-effacing."

My youngest brother Pete, who is a wonderful writer, commented that he knew I must have meant *something* (he had no idea what), and that he'd even tried a Schmitt-Wagner wine once, but that his review was along the lines of: "Goes good w/chicken salad."

If you follow the advice above, your notes will be as meaningful as Pete's, only more detailed.

POSTSCRIPT

I was a drawing student at the Philadelphia College of Art when I found wine by accident. A classmate who was working his way through school as a waiter in a fashionable French restaurant somehow convinced the owners that I'd make a good busboy, despite my utter lack of experience. I'm not sure he was right, but they needed a warm body to clear tables, and I needed the job. It only took me a week or so to realize that I'd stumbled onto something wonderful. I was especially attracted to the wines, which I desperately wanted to understand, and which seemed so mysterious.

So I read wine books. Some of them, I found, merely catalog wine, giving less joy than others, which illuminate it. Of the latter, Matt Kramer's *Making Sense of Wine* and the introduction to Kermit Lynch's *Adventures on the Wine Route* should be required reading for everyone. But I didn't learn about wine from books, and neither will you. What I've come to believe about wine is the result of long experience, which is a more respectable way of saying, "lifelong habit." And I'm convinced of this much: that habits form preferences, and that good habits form better preferences. So I drink good, inexpensive wine every day, always with food, and I learn something from every bottle. You can do the same. Your first lesson is outlined on the next page.

TEACHING YOURSELF ABOUT WINE

DETAILED JOURNAL ENTRIES

WINE IDENTITY

THE PLACE

THE HUMAN CONTENT

THE GRAPES

THE VINTAGE   HOW FRESH IS IT?

WITH WHOM?

TASTING ENVIRONMENT

SERVING TEMPERATURE

WITH WHAT FOOD?

THE PRICE   WHERE PURCHASED

APPEARANCE

CLARITY   COLOR

OTHER OBSERVATIONS

NOSE

CLEANNESS   INTENSITY

DESCRIPTION

EVOLUTION

PALATE

SWEETNESS   ACIDITY

TANNIN   BODY

BALANCE

AROMA IN THE MOUTH

FINISH

QUALITY

LENGTH

37

LABEL

WINE IDENTITY

THE PLACE

THE HUMAN CONTENT

THE GRAPES

THE VINTAGE   HOW FRESH IS IT?

WITH WHOM?

TASTING ENVIRONMENT

SERVING TEMPERATURE

WITH WHAT FOOD?

THE PRICE   WHERE PURCHASED

APPEARANCE

CLARITY   COLOR

OTHER OBSERVATIONS

NOSE

CLEANNESS   INTENSITY

DESCRIPTION

EVOLUTION

PALATE

SWEETNESS   ACIDITY

TANNIN   BODY

BALANCE

AROMA IN THE MOUTH

FINISH

QUALITY

LENGTH

CONCLUSIONS & OBSERVATIONS

LABEL

WINE IDENTITY

THE PLACE ....

THE HUMAN CONTENT ....

THE GRAPES ....

THE VINTAGE .... HOW FRESH IS IT? ....

WITH WHOM? ....

TASTING ENVIRONMENT ....

SERVING TEMPERATURE ....

WITH WHAT FOOD? ....

THE PRICE .... WHERE PURCHASED ....

APPEARANCE

CLARITY .... COLOR ....

OTHER OBSERVATIONS ....

....

NOSE

CLEANNESS .... INTENSITY ....

DESCRIPTION ....

....

EVOLUTION ....

....

PALATE

SWEETNESS .... ACIDITY ....

TANNIN .... BODY ....

BALANCE ....

AROMA IN THE MOUTH ....

....

....

....

FINISH

QUALITY ....

....

LENGTH ....

....

LABEL

WINE IDENTITY

The place ....

The human content ....

The grapes ....

The vintage .... How fresh is it? ....

With whom? ....

Tasting environment ....

Serving temperature ....

With what food? ....

The price .... Where purchased ....

APPEARANCE

Clarity .... Color ....

Other observations ....

NOSE

Cleanness .... Intensity ....

Description ....

....

Evolution ....

....

PALATE

Sweetness .... Acidity ....

Tannin .... Body ....

Balance ....

Aroma in the mouth ....

....

....

....

FINISH

Quality ....

....

Length ....

....

CONCLUSIONS & OBSERVATIONS

LABEL

WINE IDENTITY

The place ....

The human content ....

The grapes ....

The vintage .... How fresh is it? ....

With whom? ....

Tasting environment ....

Serving temperature ....

With what food? ....

The price .... Where purchased ....

APPEARANCE

Clarity .... Color ....

Other observations ....

....

NOSE

Cleanness .... Intensity ....

Description ....

....

....

Evolution ....

....

PALATE

Sweetness .... Acidity ....

Tannin .... Body ....

Balance ....

Aroma in the mouth ....

....

....

....

FINISH

Quality ....

....

....

Length ....

....

LABEL

WINE IDENTITY

The place ....

The human content ....

The grapes ....

The vintage .... How fresh is it? ....

With whom? ....

Tasting environment ....

Serving temperature ....

With what food? ....

The price .... Where purchased ....

APPEARANCE

Clarity .... Color ....

Other observations ....

....

NOSE

Cleanness .... Intensity ....

Description ....

....

Evolution ....

....

PALATE

Sweetness .... Acidity ....

Tannin .... Body ....

Balance ....

Aroma in the mouth ....

....

....

....

FINISH

Quality ....

....

Length ....

....

47

LABEL

WINE IDENTITY

The place ....

The human content ....

The grapes ....

The vintage .... How fresh is it? ....

With whom? ....

Tasting environment ....

Serving temperature ....

With what food? ....

The price .... Where purchased ....

APPEARANCE

Clarity .... Color ....

Other observations ....

....

NOSE

Cleanness .... Intensity ....

Description ....

....

Evolution ....

....

PALATE

Sweetness .... Acidity ....

Tannin .... Body ....

Balance ....

Aroma in the mouth ....

....

....

....

FINISH

Quality ....

....

....

Length ....

....

CONCLUSIONS & OBSERVATIONS

LABEL

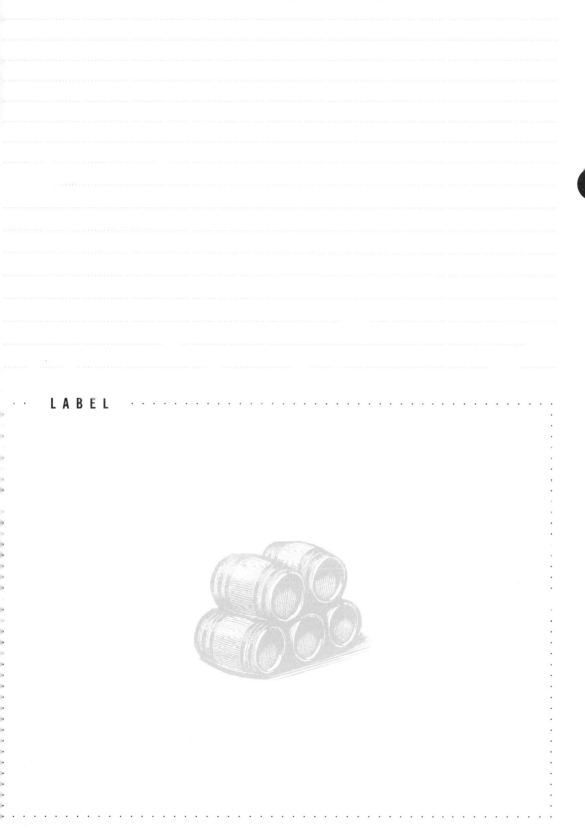

WINE IDENTITY

THE PLACE ....

THE HUMAN CONTENT ....

THE GRAPES ....

THE VINTAGE   HOW FRESH IS IT? ....

WITH WHOM? ....

TASTING ENVIRONMENT ....

SERVING TEMPERATURE ....

WITH WHAT FOOD? ....

THE PRICE ....   WHERE PURCHASED ....

APPEARANCE

CLARITY ....   COLOR ....

OTHER OBSERVATIONS ....

....

NOSE

CLEANNESS ....   INTENSITY ....

DESCRIPTION ....

....

....

EVOLUTION ....

....

PALATE

SWEETNESS ....   ACIDITY ....

TANNIN ....   BODY ....

BALANCE ....

AROMA IN THE MOUTH ....

....

....

....

FINISH

QUALITY ....

....

....

LENGTH ....

....

51

LABEL

WINE IDENTITY

THE PLACE

THE HUMAN CONTENT

THE GRAPES

THE VINTAGE   HOW FRESH IS IT?

WITH WHOM?

TASTING ENVIRONMENT

SERVING TEMPERATURE

WITH WHAT FOOD?

THE PRICE   WHERE PURCHASED

APPEARANCE

CLARITY   COLOR

OTHER OBSERVATIONS

NOSE

CLEANNESS   INTENSITY

DESCRIPTION

EVOLUTION

PALATE

SWEETNESS   ACIDITY

TANNIN   BODY

BALANCE

AROMA IN THE MOUTH

FINISH

QUALITY

LENGTH

LABEL

WINE IDENTITY

The place

The human content

The grapes

The vintage   How fresh is it?

With whom?

Tasting environment

Serving temperature

With what food?

The price   Where purchased

APPEARANCE

Clarity   Color

Other observations

NOSE

Cleanness   Intensity

Description

Evolution

PALATE

Sweetness   Acidity

Tannin   Body

Balance

Aroma in the mouth

FINISH

Quality

Length

CONCLUSIONS & OBSERVATIONS

LABEL

WINE IDENTITY

The place ....

The human content ....

The grapes ....

The vintage   How fresh is it? ....

With whom? ....

Tasting environment ....

Serving temperature ....

With what food? ....

The price   Where purchased ....

APPEARANCE

Clarity .... Color ....

Other observations ....

NOSE

Cleanness .... Intensity ....

Description ....

....

Evolution ....

PALATE

Sweetness .... Acidity ....

Tannin .... Body ....

Balance ....

Aroma in the mouth ....

....

....

FINISH

Quality ....

....

Length ....

....

56

CONCLUSIONS & OBSERVATIONS

LABEL

WINE IDENTITY

The place ....

The human content ....

The grapes ....

The vintage .... How fresh is it? ....

With whom? ....

Tasting environment ....

Serving temperature ....

With what food? ....

The price .... Where purchased ....

APPEARANCE

Clarity .... Color ....

Other observations ....

NOSE

Cleanness .... Intensity ....

Description ....

....

Evolution ....

....

PALATE

Sweetness .... Acidity ....

Tannin .... Body ....

Balance ....

Aroma in the mouth ....

....

....

FINISH

Quality ....

....

Length ....

....

58

LABEL

WINE IDENTITY

The place ....

The human content ....

The grapes ....

The vintage   How fresh is it? ....

With whom? ....

Tasting environment ....

Serving temperature ....

With what food? ....

The price   Where purchased ....

APPEARANCE

Clarity .... Color ....

Other observations ....

NOSE

Cleanness .... Intensity ....

Description ....

....

Evolution ....

PALATE

Sweetness .... Acidity ....

Tannin .... Body ....

Balance ....

Aroma in the mouth ....

....

....

FINISH

Quality ....

....

Length ....

....

LABEL

WINE IDENTITY

The place ....

The human content ....

The grapes ....

The vintage .... How fresh is it? ....

With whom? ....

Tasting environment ....

Serving temperature ....

With what food? ....

The price .... Where purchased ....

APPEARANCE

Clarity .... Color ....

Other observations ....

....

NOSE

Cleanness .... Intensity ....

Description ....

....

Evolution ....

....

PALATE

Sweetness .... Acidity ....

Tannin .... Body ....

Balance ....

Aroma in the mouth ....

....

....

FINISH

Quality ....

....

Length ....

....

63

LABEL

WINE IDENTITY

The place ....

The human content ....

The grapes ....

The vintage .... How fresh is it? ....

With whom? ....

Tasting environment ....

Serving temperature ....

With what food? ....

The price .... Where purchased ....

APPEARANCE

Clarity .... Color ....

Other observations ....

NOSE

Cleanness .... Intensity ....

Description ....

....

....

Evolution ....

....

PALATE

Sweetness .... Acidity ....

Tannin .... Body ....

Balance ....

Aroma in the mouth ....

....

....

....

FINISH

Quality ....

....

....

Length ....

CONCLUSIONS & OBSERVATIONS

LABEL

WINE IDENTITY

The place ....

The human content ....

The grapes ....

The vintage .... How fresh is it? ....

With whom? ....

Tasting environment ....

Serving temperature ....

With what food? ....

The price .... Where purchased ....

APPEARANCE

Clarity .... Color ....

Other observations ....

....

NOSE

Cleanness .... Intensity ....

Description ....

....

....

Evolution ....

....

PALATE

Sweetness .... Acidity ....

Tannin .... Body ....

Balance ....

Aroma in the mouth ....

....

....

....

FINISH

Quality ....

....

....

Length ....

....

CONCLUSIONS & OBSERVATIONS

LABEL

WINE IDENTITY

The place ....

The human content ....

The grapes ....

The vintage .... How fresh is it? ....

With whom? ....

Tasting environment ....

Serving temperature ....

With what food? ....

The price .... Where purchased ....

APPEARANCE

Clarity .... Color ....

Other observations ....

....

NOSE

Cleanness .... Intensity ....

Description ....

....

Evolution ....

....

PALATE

Sweetness .... Acidity ....

Tannin .... Body ....

Balance ....

Aroma in the mouth ....

....

....

....

FINISH

Quality ....

....

Length ....

....

CONCLUSIONS & OBSERVATIONS

LABEL

WINE IDENTITY

The place

The human content

The grapes

The vintage   How fresh is it?

With whom?

Tasting environment

Serving temperature

With what food?

70

The price   Where purchased

APPEARANCE

Clarity   Color

Other observations

NOSE

Cleanness   Intensity

Description

Evolution

PALATE

Sweetness   Acidity

Tannin   Body

Balance

Aroma in the mouth

FINISH

Quality

Length

LABEL

WINE IDENTITY

THE PLACE ....

THE HUMAN CONTENT ....

THE GRAPES ....

THE VINTAGE .... HOW FRESH IS IT? ....

WITH WHOM? ....

TASTING ENVIRONMENT ....

SERVING TEMPERATURE ....

WITH WHAT FOOD? ....

THE PRICE .... WHERE PURCHASED ....

APPEARANCE

CLARITY .... COLOR ....

OTHER OBSERVATIONS ....

NOSE

CLEANNESS .... INTENSITY ....

DESCRIPTION ....

....

EVOLUTION ....

PALATE

SWEETNESS .... ACIDITY ....

TANNIN .... BODY ....

BALANCE ....

AROMA IN THE MOUTH ....

....

....

FINISH

QUALITY ....

....

LENGTH ....

72

73

LABEL

WINE IDENTITY

The place

The human content

The grapes

The vintage   How fresh is it?

With whom?

Tasting environment

Serving temperature

With what food?

The price   Where purchased

APPEARANCE

Clarity   Color

Other observations

NOSE

Cleanness   Intensity

Description

Evolution

PALATE

Sweetness   Acidity

Tannin   Body

Balance

Aroma in the mouth

FINISH

Quality

Length

CONCLUSIONS & OBSERVATIONS

LABEL

WINE IDENTITY

The place

The human content

The grapes

The vintage   How fresh is it?

With whom?

Tasting environment

Serving temperature

With what food?

The price   Where purchased

APPEARANCE

Clarity   Color

Other observations

NOSE

Cleanness   Intensity

Description

Evolution

PALATE

Sweetness   Acidity

Tannin   Body

Balance

Aroma in the mouth

FINISH

Quality

Length

CONCLUSIONS & OBSERVATIONS

LABEL

WINE IDENTITY

The place ....

The human content ....

The grapes ....

The vintage .... How fresh is it? ....

With whom? ....

Tasting environment ....

Serving temperature ....

With what food? ....

The price .... Where purchased ....

APPEARANCE

Clarity .... Color ....

Other observations ....

....

NOSE

Cleanness .... Intensity ....

Description ....

....

....

Evolution ....

....

PALATE

Sweetness .... Acidity ....

Tannin .... Body ....

Balance ....

Aroma in the mouth ....

....

....

....

FINISH

Quality ....

....

....

Length ....

....

CONCLUSIONS & OBSERVATIONS

LABEL

80

TEACHING YOURSELF ABOUT WINE

OTHER WINES TO REMEMBER

WINE IDENTITY

THE PLACE

THE HUMAN CONTENT

THE GRAPES   THE VINTAGE   HOW FRESH IS IT?

THE PRICE   WHERE PURCHASED

APPEARANCE

CLARITY   COLOR

OTHER OBSERVATIONS

NOSE

CLEANNESS   INTENSITY

DESCRIPTION

PALATE

SWEETNESS   ACIDITY   TANNIN

BODY   AROMA IN THE MOUTH

FINISH

CONCLUSIONS

WINE IDENTITY

THE PLACE

THE HUMAN CONTENT

THE GRAPES   THE VINTAGE   HOW FRESH IS IT?

THE PRICE   WHERE PURCHASED

APPEARANCE

CLARITY   COLOR

OTHER OBSERVATIONS

NOSE

CLEANNESS   INTENSITY

DESCRIPTION

PALATE

SWEETNESS   ACIDITY   TANNIN

BODY   AROMA IN THE MOUTH

FINISH

CONCLUSIONS

OF WINE AND ROSÉS

When spring arrives in Philadelphia, the arrival of the new vintage of Provence rosés is as welcome as the warmer weather and its promise of the summer grill. Made from black grapes like Syrah, Grenache, and Cabernet Sauvignon, rosé is a specialty of Provence, where it does the work of aromatic dry white wine in an area that has great seafood but doesn't have good white grapes.

It could hardly be less fashionable, but I for one *love* good pink wine. And self-proclaimed "connoisseurs" (who think they demonstrate their sophistication by professing to disdain rosés) are probably only afraid someone might see their glass and think they're drinking white Zinfandel.

The fact is, nothing would demonstrate more emphatically their *genuine* sophistication than to be seen drinking the local rosé alongside a *bourride de poisson* in a St. Tropez bistro. Drunk as young and as fresh as possible, good Provence rosé is just as delicious with grilled chicken in Philadelphia.

WINE IDENTITY

THE PLACE

THE HUMAN CONTENT

THE GRAPES   THE VINTAGE   HOW FRESH IS IT?

THE PRICE   WHERE PURCHASED

APPEARANCE

CLARITY   COLOR

OTHER OBSERVATIONS

NOSE

CLEANNESS   INTENSITY

DESCRIPTION

PALATE

SWEETNESS   ACIDITY   TANNIN

BODY   AROMA IN THE MOUTH

FINISH

CONCLUSIONS

WINE IDENTITY

THE PLACE

THE HUMAN CONTENT

THE GRAPES   THE VINTAGE   HOW FRESH IS IT?

THE PRICE   WHERE PURCHASED

APPEARANCE

CLARITY   COLOR

OTHER OBSERVATIONS

NOSE

CLEANNESS   INTENSITY

DESCRIPTION

PALATE

SWEETNESS   ACIDITY   TANNIN

BODY   AROMA IN THE MOUTH

FINISH

CONCLUSIONS

CORKY WINE

Have you ever tasted a wine that was *corked*? And I don't mean one you needed a corkscrew to open. I mean a bottle of wine spoiled by trichloroanisole, or TCA, which comes from infected corks.

TCA is formed when the bleaching agent used to disinfect corks is metabolized by a common mold. It has a musty, wet cardboard smell that's detectable at very low concentrations, and corked bottles never improve. They should always be sent back in restaurants.

By the way, nothing you see on the cork, including black, greasy mold under the capsule, has anything to do with corked wine. In fact, mold on the cellar end of the cork is usually a *good* sign that the wine was stored properly in a cool, humid cellar. The only thing you never want to see under the capsule is wine that has leaked because of heat.

It's estimated that as much as 5 percent of the world's harvest is damaged to some degree by TCA. Which leads to an obvious question: with so many other options available, why do we still use corks? I for one will celebrate when Château Lafite-Rothschild offers a special archival bottling (at a higher price, if necessary), in a revolutionary new format...complete with a tight aluminum screw cap.

WINE IDENTITY

The place

The human content

The grapes   The vintage   How fresh is it?

The price   Where purchased

APPEARANCE

Clarity   Color

Other observations

NOSE

Cleanness   Intensity

Description

PALATE

Sweetness   Acidity   Tannin

Body   Aroma in the mouth

Finish

CONCLUSIONS

WINE IDENTITY

The place

The human content

The grapes   The vintage   How fresh is it?

The price   Where purchased

APPEARANCE

Clarity   Color

Other observations

NOSE

Cleanness   Intensity

Description

PALATE

Sweetness   Acidity   Tannin

Body   Aroma in the mouth

Finish

CONCLUSIONS

WINE IDENTITY

The place ....
The human content ....
The grapes .... The vintage .... How fresh is it? ....
The price .... Where purchased ....

APPEARANCE

Clarity .... Color ....
Other observations ....

NOSE

Cleanness .... Intensity ....
Description ....

PALATE

Sweetness .... Acidity .... Tannin ....
Body .... Aroma in the mouth ....
Finish ....

CONCLUSIONS

WINE IDENTITY

The place ....
The human content ....
The grapes .... The vintage .... How fresh is it? ....
The price .... Where purchased ....

APPEARANCE

Clarity .... Color ....
Other observations ....

NOSE

Cleanness .... Intensity ....
Description ....

PALATE

Sweetness .... Acidity .... Tannin ....
Body .... Aroma in the mouth ....
Finish ....

CONCLUSIONS

WINE IDENTITY

THE PLACE ....

THE HUMAN CONTENT ....

THE GRAPES .... THE VINTAGE .... HOW FRESH IS IT? ....

THE PRICE .... WHERE PURCHASED ....

APPEARANCE

CLARITY .... COLOR ....

OTHER OBSERVATIONS ....

NOSE

CLEANNESS .... INTENSITY ....

DESCRIPTION ....

PALATE

SWEETNESS .... ACIDITY .... TANNIN ....

BODY .... AROMA IN THE MOUTH ....

FINISH ....

CONCLUSIONS

....

WINE IDENTITY

THE PLACE ....

THE HUMAN CONTENT ....

THE GRAPES .... THE VINTAGE .... HOW FRESH IS IT? ....

THE PRICE .... WHERE PURCHASED ....

APPEARANCE

CLARITY .... COLOR ....

OTHER OBSERVATIONS ....

NOSE

CLEANNESS .... INTENSITY ....

DESCRIPTION ....

PALATE

SWEETNESS .... ACIDITY .... TANNIN ....

BODY .... AROMA IN THE MOUTH ....

FINISH ....

CONCLUSIONS

....

A STAR THROWER

The Romans planted grapes on the Ayler Kupp because that was where the snow melted first in the early spring. It would, arguably, be the world's most beautiful vineyard, lush with the deep green foliage of well-tended vines in July, if only the orderly rows didn't alternate between black slate moonscapes and the wild tangle of abandoned vineyard, where the labor is too expensive to justify the production of the classic Rieslings that grow there. The wines sell too cheaply. Producers like Johann Peter Reinert in Kanzem, who makes wine from the Ayler Kupp, are like the Star Thrower in Loren Eiselys's *The Unexpected Universe*, who rescues stranded starfish one by one by throwing them back into the surf that washed them up. Reinert does the same for his vines: he carries the earth back up the hill every time it washes down.

The following are not expressions of arguable opinion; they are wine facts:

1. At the end of the nineteenth century, British aristocrats regularly paid about one and a half times the price of Château Lafite-Rothschild for fine German Reislings

2. "Chardonnay" is not a synonym for white wine.

3. Dry wine doesn't mean good wine, nor does drier wine mean better wine.

4. "Riesling" doesn't mean sweet.

WINE IDENTITY

THE PLACE

THE HUMAN CONTENT

THE GRAPES   THE VINTAGE   HOW FRESH IS IT?

THE PRICE   WHERE PURCHASED

APPEARANCE

CLARITY   COLOR

OTHER OBSERVATIONS

NOSE

CLEANNESS   INTENSITY

DESCRIPTION

PALATE

SWEETNESS   ACIDITY   TANNIN

BODY   AROMA IN THE MOUTH

FINISH

CONCLUSIONS

WINE IDENTITY

THE PLACE

THE HUMAN CONTENT

THE GRAPES   THE VINTAGE   HOW FRESH IS IT?

THE PRICE   WHERE PURCHASED

APPEARANCE

CLARITY   COLOR

OTHER OBSERVATIONS

NOSE

CLEANNESS   INTENSITY

DESCRIPTION

PALATE

SWEETNESS   ACIDITY   TANNIN

BODY   AROMA IN THE MOUTH

FINISH

CONCLUSIONS

A WINE PRESERVATION SYSTEM

Twenty years ago I was invited to a wine tasting where an expensive, new nitrogen-displacement wine preservation system was being introduced. The object was to demonstrate that open wine kept for two weeks attached to the device tasted the same as wine opened only two hours before. I wasn't impressed. I thought it was easy to tell which wine was which.

Besides, I had my own system for preserving open bottles that worked better and cost less. Here's how to use it: As soon as you pull the cork, immediately pour what you won't use into a smaller glass container. A ten-ounce glass soda bottle with a good plastic screw cap is ideal, but I've used Snapple jars and aspirin bottles, too. Fill it all the way to the top, put it in the refrigerator, and the wine will last for weeks.

But I rarely go to the trouble anymore. I just finish the bottle.

WINE IDENTITY

The place

The human content

The grapes .... The vintage .... How fresh is it?

The price .... Where purchased

APPEARANCE

Clarity .... Color

Other observations

NOSE

Cleanness .... Intensity

Description

PALATE

Sweetness .... Acidity .... Tannin

Body .... Aroma in the mouth

Finish

CONCLUSIONS

WINE IDENTITY

The place

The human content

The grapes .... The vintage .... How fresh is it?

The price .... Where purchased

APPEARANCE

Clarity .... Color

Other observations

NOSE

Cleanness .... Intensity

Description

PALATE

Sweetness .... Acidity .... Tannin

Body .... Aroma in the mouth

Finish

CONCLUSIONS

WINE IDENTITY

THE PLACE

THE HUMAN CONTENT

THE GRAPES   THE VINTAGE   HOW FRESH IS IT?

THE PRICE   WHERE PURCHASED

APPEARANCE

CLARITY   COLOR

OTHER OBSERVATIONS

NOSE

CLEANNESS   INTENSITY

DESCRIPTION

PALATE

SWEETNESS   ACIDITY   TANNIN

BODY   AROMA IN THE MOUTH

FINISH

CONCLUSIONS

WINE IDENTITY

THE PLACE

THE HUMAN CONTENT

THE GRAPES   THE VINTAGE   HOW FRESH IS IT?

THE PRICE   WHERE PURCHASED

APPEARANCE

CLARITY   COLOR

OTHER OBSERVATIONS

NOSE

CLEANNESS   INTENSITY

DESCRIPTION

PALATE

SWEETNESS   ACIDITY   TANNIN

BODY   AROMA IN THE MOUTH

FINISH

CONCLUSIONS

WINE IDENTITY

THE PLACE

THE HUMAN CONTENT

THE GRAPES   THE VINTAGE   HOW FRESH IS IT?

THE PRICE   WHERE PURCHASED

APPEARANCE

CLARITY   COLOR

OTHER OBSERVATIONS

NOSE

CLEANNESS   INTENSITY

DESCRIPTION

PALATE

SWEETNESS   ACIDITY   TANNIN

BODY   AROMA IN THE MOUTH

FINISH

CONCLUSIONS

WINE IDENTITY

THE PLACE

THE HUMAN CONTENT

THE GRAPES   THE VINTAGE   HOW FRESH IS IT?

THE PRICE   WHERE PURCHASED

APPEARANCE

CLARITY   COLOR

OTHER OBSERVATIONS

NOSE

CLEANNESS   INTENSITY

DESCRIPTION

PALATE

SWEETNESS   ACIDITY   TANNIN

BODY   AROMA IN THE MOUTH

FINISH

CONCLUSIONS

CHAMPAGNE

Long before the wide availability of bottles and corks made the accidental discovery of sparkling wine possible, the wines of Champagne were counted among the finest in France. Like the wines of Burgundy, with which they competed for the world's attention, they were red and white still wines made from Pinot Noir and Chardonnay. And like Burgundy, they were (and are) as variable in quality: the best wines fine and elegant; the worst unripe and rotten.

Today the wines of Champagne are made sparkling by a particularly difficult and expensive method, and any competition with Burgundy is ancient history. But they're also mostly blended wines, made in huge quantities by merchant producers with famous names, most of whom grow only a small portion of the grapes used in their wines. Because of worldwide demand, Champagne is now a mass-produced commodity. Some of the fruit is second-rate at best, and Champagne as a region routinely delivers some of the poorest expensive wine made anywhere.

Of course there's great wine in Champagne too, and I go out of my way to drink it whenever I can. I once attended a Davidoff cigar tasting hosted by the Baroness Philippine de Rothschild at the Four Seasons Hotel only because they were pouring Krug 1982.

WINE IDENTITY

THE PLACE ....

THE HUMAN CONTENT ....

THE GRAPES .... THE VINTAGE .... HOW FRESH IS IT? ....

THE PRICE .... WHERE PURCHASED ....

APPEARANCE

CLARITY .... COLOR ....

OTHER OBSERVATIONS ....

NOSE

CLEANNESS .... INTENSITY ....

DESCRIPTION ....

PALATE

SWEETNESS .... ACIDITY .... TANNIN ....

BODY .... AROMA IN THE MOUTH ....

FINISH ....

CONCLUSIONS

....

....

WINE IDENTITY

THE PLACE ....

THE HUMAN CONTENT ....

THE GRAPES .... THE VINTAGE .... HOW FRESH IS IT? ....

THE PRICE .... WHERE PURCHASED ....

APPEARANCE

CLARITY .... COLOR ....

OTHER OBSERVATIONS ....

NOSE

CLEANNESS .... INTENSITY ....

DESCRIPTION ....

PALATE

SWEETNESS .... ACIDITY .... TANNIN ....

BODY .... AROMA IN THE MOUTH ....

FINISH ....

CONCLUSIONS

A TOUCH OF CLASSIFICATION

In the Médoc, where some of the finest Bordeaux wines grow, there is an official hierarchy of estates, drawn up by Bordeaux brokers in 1855. It ranks the estates based on the prices their wines commanded in the open market at the time. Known as the Official Classification of the Wines of the Gironde of 1855, it included sixty-one estates in the Médoc plus one Graves (Château Haut-Brion); and, in a separate listing, twenty-six estates that produce the sweet wines of Sauternes-Barsac. The red wine estates were ranked in five classes. At the top were the First Growths, which included Châteaux Lafite-Rothschild, Latour, Margaux, and Haut-Brion. The remaining classified growths were ranked as Second, Third, Fourth, and Fifth Growths.

The Classification is a remarkably durable document that has been modified only once. In 1973, after nearly fifty years of intense lobbying by its owner, Château Mouton-Rothschild was elevated from Second to First Growth. Part of the success of the classification undoubtedly lies in its appeal to the sense of order that casual, affluent wine consumers have craved.

WINE IDENTITY

THE PLACE

THE HUMAN CONTENT

THE GRAPES   THE VINTAGE   HOW FRESH IS IT?

THE PRICE   WHERE PURCHASED

APPEARANCE

CLARITY   COLOR

OTHER OBSERVATIONS

NOSE

CLEANNESS   INTENSITY

DESCRIPTION

PALATE

SWEETNESS   ACIDITY   TANNIN

BODY   AROMA IN THE MOUTH

FINISH

CONCLUSIONS

WINE IDENTITY

THE PLACE

THE HUMAN CONTENT

THE GRAPES   THE VINTAGE   HOW FRESH IS IT?

THE PRICE   WHERE PURCHASED

APPEARANCE

CLARITY   COLOR

OTHER OBSERVATIONS

NOSE

CLEANNESS   INTENSITY

DESCRIPTION

PALATE

SWEETNESS   ACIDITY   TANNIN

BODY   AROMA IN THE MOUTH

FINISH

CONCLUSIONS

WINE IDENTITY

The place ....

The human content ....

The grapes .... The vintage .... How fresh is it? ....

The price .... Where purchased ....

APPEARANCE

Clarity .... Color ....

Other observations ....

NOSE

Cleanness .... Intensity ....

Description ....

PALATE

Sweetness .... Acidity .... Tannin ....

Body .... Aroma in the mouth ....

Finish ....

CONCLUSIONS

....

WINE IDENTITY

The place ....

The human content ....

The grapes .... The vintage .... How fresh is it? ....

The price .... Where purchased ....

APPEARANCE

Clarity .... Color ....

Other observations ....

NOSE

Cleanness .... Intensity ....

Description ....

PALATE

Sweetness .... Acidity .... Tannin ....

Body .... Aroma in the mouth ....

Finish ....

CONCLUSIONS

WINE IDENTITY

The place ....

The human content ....

The grapes .... The vintage .... How fresh is it? ....

The price .... Where purchased ....

APPEARANCE

Clarity .... Color ....

Other observations ....

NOSE

Cleanness .... Intensity ....

Description ....

PALATE

Sweetness .... Acidity .... Tannin ....

Body .... Aroma in the mouth ....

Finish ....

CONCLUSIONS

....

WINE IDENTITY

The place ....

The human content ....

The grapes .... The vintage .... How fresh is it? ....

The price .... Where purchased ....

APPEARANCE

Clarity .... Color ....

Other observations ....

NOSE

Cleanness .... Intensity ....

Description ....

PALATE

Sweetness .... Acidity .... Tannin ....

Body .... Aroma in the mouth ....

Finish ....

CONCLUSIONS

....

LIVING, BREATHING WINE

Because every one of the aromatic compounds in a glass of wine has its own molecular weight and vapor pressure, its measurable concentration is different every time we take a sip. And because wine rapidly absorbs oxygen as soon as it's exposed to air, new aromatics are actually being formed as soon as the wine is poured. We observe, if we pay attention, that good wine is always changing in the glass.

Which is exactly is why I *never* recommend opening wine early to let it "breathe." Wine doesn't simply "improve" or "soften" or "mellow" after it's opened. It evolves in the glass, in a way that actively engages us in its vitality. That's what makes it different from everything else we drink.

But I hear the complaint all the time. "Greg, we should have let the wine breathe. It just kept getting better, and better, and better, and better. And then it was gone!"

Then again, life should be like that, shouldn't it?

WINE IDENTITY

THE PLACE

THE HUMAN CONTENT

THE GRAPES   THE VINTAGE   HOW FRESH IS IT?

THE PRICE   WHERE PURCHASED

APPEARANCE

CLARITY   COLOR

OTHER OBSERVATIONS

NOSE

CLEANNESS   INTENSITY

DESCRIPTION

PALATE

SWEETNESS   ACIDITY   TANNIN

BODY   AROMA IN THE MOUTH

FINISH

CONCLUSIONS

WINE IDENTITY

THE PLACE

THE HUMAN CONTENT

THE GRAPES   THE VINTAGE   HOW FRESH IS IT?

THE PRICE   WHERE PURCHASED

APPEARANCE

CLARITY   COLOR

OTHER OBSERVATIONS

NOSE

CLEANNESS   INTENSITY

DESCRIPTION

PALATE

SWEETNESS   ACIDITY   TANNIN

BODY   AROMA IN THE MOUTH

FINISH

CONCLUSIONS

WINE IDENTITY

The place

The human content

The grapes   The vintage   How fresh is it?

The price   Where purchased

APPEARANCE

Clarity   Color

Other observations

NOSE

Cleanness   Intensity

Description

PALATE

Sweetness   Acidity   Tannin

Body   Aroma in the mouth

Finish

CONCLUSIONS

WINE IDENTITY

The place

The human content

The grapes   The vintage   How fresh is it?

The price   Where purchased

APPEARANCE

Clarity   Color

Other observations

NOSE

Cleanness   Intensity

Description

PALATE

Sweetness   Acidity   Tannin

Body   Aroma in the mouth

Finish

CONCLUSIONS

WINE IDENTITY

THE PLACE ....

THE HUMAN CONTENT ....

THE GRAPES .... THE VINTAGE .... HOW FRESH IS IT? ....

THE PRICE .... WHERE PURCHASED ....

APPEARANCE

CLARITY .... COLOR ....

OTHER OBSERVATIONS ....

NOSE

CLEANNESS .... INTENSITY ....

DESCRIPTION ....

PALATE

SWEETNESS .... ACIDITY .... TANNIN ....

BODY .... AROMA IN THE MOUTH ....

FINISH ....

CONCLUSIONS
....

WINE IDENTITY

THE PLACE ....

THE HUMAN CONTENT ....

THE GRAPES .... THE VINTAGE .... HOW FRESH IS IT? ....

THE PRICE .... WHERE PURCHASED ....

APPEARANCE

CLARITY .... COLOR ....

OTHER OBSERVATIONS ....

NOSE

CLEANNESS .... INTENSITY ....

DESCRIPTION ....

PALATE

SWEETNESS .... ACIDITY .... TANNIN ....

BODY .... AROMA IN THE MOUTH ....

FINISH ....

CONCLUSIONS
....

CONTAINS SULFITES

"I had this wine at Georges Blanc," a customer huffed one day, "and in France it didn't have sulfites in it."

Well, sometimes the customer's wrong. All wine contains sulfites...even organic wine and biodynamic wine. The only difference between the bottle he drank in Vonnas and the one I'm serving him is what's printed on the label. "Contains Sulfites" is the warning required by the U.S. government that ostensibly protects asthmatics who may be profoundly allergic to these otherwise perfectly harmless substances.

WINE IDENTITY

THE PLACE

THE HUMAN CONTENT

THE GRAPES   THE VINTAGE   HOW FRESH IS IT?

THE PRICE   WHERE PURCHASED

APPEARANCE

CLARITY   COLOR

OTHER OBSERVATIONS

NOSE

CLEANNESS   INTENSITY

DESCRIPTION

PALATE

SWEETNESS   ACIDITY   TANNIN

BODY   AROMA IN THE MOUTH

FINISH

CONCLUSIONS

WINE IDENTITY

THE PLACE

THE HUMAN CONTENT

THE GRAPES   THE VINTAGE   HOW FRESH IS IT?

THE PRICE   WHERE PURCHASED

APPEARANCE

CLARITY   COLOR

OTHER OBSERVATIONS

NOSE

CLEANNESS   INTENSITY

DESCRIPTION

PALATE

SWEETNESS   ACIDITY   TANNIN

BODY   AROMA IN THE MOUTH

FINISH

CONCLUSIONS

WINE IDENTITY

THE PLACE

THE HUMAN CONTENT

THE GRAPES   THE VINTAGE   HOW FRESH IS IT?

THE PRICE   WHERE PURCHASED

APPEARANCE

CLARITY   COLOR

OTHER OBSERVATIONS

NOSE

CLEANNESS   INTENSITY

DESCRIPTION

PALATE

SWEETNESS   ACIDITY   TANNIN

BODY   AROMA IN THE MOUTH

FINISH

CONCLUSIONS

WINE IDENTITY

THE PLACE

THE HUMAN CONTENT

THE GRAPES   THE VINTAGE   HOW FRESH IS IT?

THE PRICE   WHERE PURCHASED

APPEARANCE

CLARITY   COLOR

OTHER OBSERVATIONS

NOSE

CLEANNESS   INTENSITY

DESCRIPTION

PALATE

SWEETNESS   ACIDITY   TANNIN

BODY   AROMA IN THE MOUTH

FINISH

CONCLUSIONS

WINE IDENTITY

THE PLACE ....

THE HUMAN CONTENT ....

THE GRAPES .... THE VINTAGE .... HOW FRESH IS IT? ....

THE PRICE .... WHERE PURCHASED ....

APPEARANCE

CLARITY .... COLOR ....

OTHER OBSERVATIONS ....

NOSE

CLEANNESS .... INTENSITY ....

DESCRIPTION ....

PALATE

SWEETNESS .... ACIDITY .... TANNIN ....

BODY .... AROMA IN THE MOUTH ....

FINISH ....

CONCLUSIONS

....
....

WINE IDENTITY

THE PLACE ....

THE HUMAN CONTENT ....

THE GRAPES .... THE VINTAGE .... HOW FRESH IS IT? ....

THE PRICE .... WHERE PURCHASED ....

APPEARANCE

CLARITY .... COLOR ....

OTHER OBSERVATIONS ....

NOSE

CLEANNESS .... INTENSITY ....

DESCRIPTION ....

PALATE

SWEETNESS .... ACIDITY .... TANNIN ....

BODY .... AROMA IN THE MOUTH ....

FINISH ....

CONCLUSIONS

....
....

STAY COOL

Here's an example of miserable wine service, which happened at an outdoor cafe in Napa fifteen years ago. Tom Selfridge, who was the Winemaker-President of Beaulieu Vineyards at the time, had invited me to lunch. We had an ongoing friendship when I was a sommelier, and my wine list at Le Bec-Fin featured several vintages of his outstanding Cabernet Sauvignon.

When the Pinot Noir he ordered arrived palpably hot, the bottle having languished in the sun on a rack above the bar, Tom very politely asked the waiter for an ice bucket. "Sir," came the haughty reply, "red wine should never be chilled."

Wrong. The most useless wine accessory you can own is a display rack for your living room or kitchen. If you use one, be sure at least to cool your red wine a bit before you serve it. Half an hour in the refrigerator should do it. But better yet, get rid of the rack. If you don't have other storage options, keep your wine in the refrigerator; and if it's red wine, just take it out a half-hour before you serve it.

WINE IDENTITY

THE PLACE ....

THE HUMAN CONTENT ....

THE GRAPES .... THE VINTAGE .... HOW FRESH IS IT? ....

THE PRICE .... WHERE PURCHASED ....

APPEARANCE

CLARITY .... COLOR ....

OTHER OBSERVATIONS ....

NOSE

CLEANNESS .... INTENSITY ....

DESCRIPTION ....

PALATE

SWEETNESS .... ACIDITY .... TANNIN ....

BODY .... AROMA IN THE MOUTH ....

FINISH ....

CONCLUSIONS ....

....

WINE IDENTITY

THE PLACE ....

THE HUMAN CONTENT ....

THE GRAPES .... THE VINTAGE .... HOW FRESH IS IT? ....

THE PRICE .... WHERE PURCHASED ....

APPEARANCE

CLARITY .... COLOR ....

OTHER OBSERVATIONS ....

NOSE

CLEANNESS .... INTENSITY ....

DESCRIPTION ....

PALATE

SWEETNESS .... ACIDITY .... TANNIN ....

BODY .... AROMA IN THE MOUTH ....

FINISH ....

CONCLUSIONS

....

WINE IDENTITY

The place ....

The human content ....

The grapes .... The vintage .... How fresh is it? ....

The price .... Where purchased ....

APPEARANCE

Clarity .... Color ....

Other observations ....

NOSE

Cleanness .... Intensity ....

Description ....

PALATE

Sweetness .... Acidity .... Tannin ....

Body .... Aroma in the mouth ....

Finish ....

CONCLUSIONS

....

....

WINE IDENTITY

The place ....

The human content ....

The grapes .... The vintage .... How fresh is it? ....

The price .... Where purchased ....

APPEARANCE

Clarity .... Color ....

Other observations ....

NOSE

Cleanness .... Intensity ....

Description ....

PALATE

Sweetness .... Acidity .... Tannin ....

Body .... Aroma in the mouth ....

Finish ....

CONCLUSIONS

WINE IDENTITY

THE PLACE

THE HUMAN CONTENT

THE GRAPES   THE VINTAGE   HOW FRESH IS IT?

THE PRICE   WHERE PURCHASED

APPEARANCE

CLARITY   COLOR

OTHER OBSERVATIONS

NOSE

CLEANNESS   INTENSITY

DESCRIPTION

PALATE

SWEETNESS   ACIDITY   TANNIN

BODY   AROMA IN THE MOUTH

FINISH

CONCLUSIONS

WINE IDENTITY

THE PLACE

THE HUMAN CONTENT

THE GRAPES   THE VINTAGE   HOW FRESH IS IT?

THE PRICE   WHERE PURCHASED

APPEARANCE

CLARITY   COLOR

OTHER OBSERVATIONS

NOSE

CLEANNESS   INTENSITY

DESCRIPTION

PALATE

SWEETNESS   ACIDITY   TANNIN

BODY   AROMA IN THE MOUTH

FINISH

CONCLUSIONS

A GREAT WINE SHOP

If you find you have genuinely developed an interest in fine wine, the best thing you can do for yourself is find a great wine shop. Here's what to look for:

First, the place is clean, which is a measure of the respect the staff has for its customers, its wines, and for itself (a dirty floor and stained labels are a bad sign, and bottles showing obvious leakage are worse). Second, it's cool inside. If it's warm enough that you're uncomfortable in your winter coat, turn around and leave. A wine shop can't be too cool. After all, wine is an agricultural product. And third, there's real selection, not just hundreds of wines.

Most important of all, a great wine shop is staffed by informed professionals who don't rely on the distributors' shelf-talkers for information about their products. They should be able to tell you something meaningful about every wine they sell. If it happens that they also have some knowledge of food, you've found a rare treasure.

WINE IDENTITY

THE PLACE ....

THE HUMAN CONTENT ....

THE GRAPES .... THE VINTAGE .... HOW FRESH IS IT? ....

THE PRICE .... WHERE PURCHASED ....

APPEARANCE

CLARITY .... COLOR ....

OTHER OBSERVATIONS ....

NOSE

CLEANNESS .... INTENSITY ....

DESCRIPTION ....

PALATE

SWEETNESS .... ACIDITY .... TANNIN ....

BODY .... AROMA IN THE MOUTH ....

FINISH ....

CONCLUSIONS ....

....

WINE IDENTITY

THE PLACE ....

THE HUMAN CONTENT ....

THE GRAPES .... THE VINTAGE .... HOW FRESH IS IT? ....

THE PRICE .... WHERE PURCHASED ....

APPEARANCE

CLARITY .... COLOR ....

OTHER OBSERVATIONS ....

NOSE

CLEANNESS .... INTENSITY ....

DESCRIPTION ....

PALATE

SWEETNESS .... ACIDITY .... TANNIN ....

BODY .... AROMA IN THE MOUTH ....

FINISH ....

CONCLUSIONS

....

WINE IDENTITY

The place ....

The human content ....

The grapes .... The vintage .... How fresh is it? ....

The price .... Where purchased ....

APPEARANCE

Clarity .... Color ....

Other observations ....

NOSE

Cleanness .... Intensity ....

Description ....

PALATE

Sweetness .... Acidity .... Tannin ....

Body .... Aroma in the mouth ....

Finish ....

CONCLUSIONS

....

....

WINE IDENTITY

The place ....

The human content ....

The grapes .... The vintage .... How fresh is it? ....

The price .... Where purchased ....

APPEARANCE

Clarity .... Color ....

Other observations ....

NOSE

Cleanness .... Intensity ....

Description ....

PALATE

Sweetness .... Acidity .... Tannin ....

Body .... Aroma in the mouth ....

Finish ....

CONCLUSIONS

WINE IDENTITY

THE PLACE

THE HUMAN CONTENT

THE GRAPES   THE VINTAGE   HOW FRESH IS IT?

THE PRICE   WHERE PURCHASED

APPEARANCE

CLARITY   COLOR

OTHER OBSERVATIONS

NOSE

CLEANNESS   INTENSITY

DESCRIPTION

PALATE

SWEETNESS   ACIDITY   TANNIN

BODY   AROMA IN THE MOUTH

FINISH

CONCLUSIONS

WINE IDENTITY

THE PLACE

THE HUMAN CONTENT

THE GRAPES   THE VINTAGE   HOW FRESH IS IT?

THE PRICE   WHERE PURCHASED

APPEARANCE

CLARITY   COLOR

OTHER OBSERVATIONS

NOSE

CLEANNESS   INTENSITY

DESCRIPTION

PALATE

SWEETNESS   ACIDITY   TANNIN

BODY   AROMA IN THE MOUTH

FINISH

CONCLUSIONS

WINE AND CHEESE

Late one night many years ago, when I was a young sommelier, I found myself faced with a full, open bottle of Château Lafite Rothschild 1945. I'd decanted it earlier for a customer who had decided to drink something else, and who generously left it for me. Common wisdom calls for the best red wine possible with cheese, so I assumed that the Lafite would be great with one of my favorites, a perfectly ripe soft cheese from the French Alps called *Reblochon*.

Well, the cheese made the wine taste thin and metallic, and the wine made the cheese taste like unmentionable organic matter. So, knowing that good Reblochon was likely to come my way more often than Lafite '45, I put away the cheese and finished the wine with bread and butter.

WINE IDENTITY

THE PLACE

THE HUMAN CONTENT

THE GRAPES   THE VINTAGE   HOW FRESH IS IT?

THE PRICE   WHERE PURCHASED

APPEARANCE

CLARITY   COLOR

OTHER OBSERVATIONS

NOSE

CLEANNESS   INTENSITY

DESCRIPTION

PALATE

SWEETNESS   ACIDITY   TANNIN

BODY   AROMA IN THE MOUTH

FINISH

CONCLUSIONS

WINE IDENTITY

THE PLACE

THE HUMAN CONTENT

THE GRAPES   THE VINTAGE   HOW FRESH IS IT?

THE PRICE   WHERE PURCHASED

APPEARANCE

CLARITY   COLOR

OTHER OBSERVATIONS

NOSE

CLEANNESS   INTENSITY

DESCRIPTION

PALATE

SWEETNESS   ACIDITY   TANNIN

BODY   AROMA IN THE MOUTH

FINISH

CONCLUSIONS

WINE IDENTITY

The place ....

The human content ....

The grapes .... The vintage .... How fresh is it? ....

The price .... Where purchased ....

APPEARANCE

Clarity .... Color ....

Other observations ....

NOSE

119

Cleanness .... Intensity ....

Description ....

PALATE

Sweetness .... Acidity .... Tannin ....

Body .... Aroma in the mouth ....

Finish ....

CONCLUSIONS

....

WINE IDENTITY

The place ....

The human content ....

The grapes .... The vintage .... How fresh is it? ....

The price .... Where purchased ....

APPEARANCE

Clarity .... Color ....

Other observations ....

NOSE

Cleanness .... Intensity ....

Description ....

PALATE

Sweetness .... Acidity .... Tannin ....

Body .... Aroma in the mouth ....

Finish ....

CONCLUSIONS

WINE IDENTITY

THE PLACE

THE HUMAN CONTENT

THE GRAPES   THE VINTAGE   HOW FRESH IS IT?

THE PRICE   WHERE PURCHASED

APPEARANCE

CLARITY   COLOR

OTHER OBSERVATIONS

NOSE

CLEANNESS   INTENSITY

DESCRIPTION

PALATE

SWEETNESS   ACIDITY   TANNIN

BODY   AROMA IN THE MOUTH

FINISH

CONCLUSIONS

WINE IDENTITY

THE PLACE

THE HUMAN CONTENT

THE GRAPES   THE VINTAGE   HOW FRESH IS IT?

THE PRICE   WHERE PURCHASED

APPEARANCE

CLARITY   COLOR

OTHER OBSERVATIONS

NOSE

CLEANNESS   INTENSITY

DESCRIPTION

PALATE

SWEETNESS   ACIDITY   TANNIN

BODY   AROMA IN THE MOUTH

FINISH

CONCLUSIONS

"WHEN SHOULD WE DRINK IT?"

In some ways, buying young, age-worthy wine is like having children. They both require confidence in a secure future. Which brings us to the big question: "When will that eighty-six Lafite be ready to drink?" And the bigger question: "When *should* we drink it?"

The experts confound us with vague advice, like "drink between 2004 and 2012," which assumes certain conditions of storage and allows for personal taste, but which also implies the hopeless notion of a "peak" of maturity, before or after which the wine may not be worth drinking at all.

But wait. We don't have children because we want to see what they'll be like when they're grown up. We have rewarding human experiences with them before they can talk, and when they're five and ten years old. Are they less rewarding than experiences we may have with them when they are adults? Of course not.

So I just drink up, even when the wine is "too young." I know too many wine collectors whose impressive wine cellars add little to their lives but anxiety.

WINE IDENTITY

The place ....

The human content ....

The grapes .... The vintage .... How fresh is it? ....

The price .... Where purchased ....

APPEARANCE

Clarity .... Color ....

Other observations ....

NOSE

Cleanness .... Intensity ....

Description ....

PALATE

Sweetness .... Acidity .... Tannin ....

Body .... Aroma in the mouth ....

Finish ....

CONCLUSIONS

....

WINE IDENTITY

The place ....

The human content ....

The grapes .... The vintage .... How fresh is it? ....

The price .... Where purchased ....

APPEARANCE

Clarity .... Color ....

Other observations ....

NOSE

Cleanness .... Intensity ....

Description ....

PALATE

Sweetness .... Acidity .... Tannin ....

Body .... Aroma in the mouth ....

Finish ....

CONCLUSIONS

....

BURGUNDY

Burgundy has never enjoyed the unqualified international success that makes Bordeaux a virtual synonym for fine French red wine. One reason is that the best Burgundy wines are made in much smaller quantities than most Bordeaux, and can never be as widely known. Another is that consumers who find comfort in the simple tidiness of Bordeaux labels (château+vintage = wine) become impatient with the more demanding labels of Burgundy. The problem is that there are so many appellations in Burgundy, and that each appellation may be the source of dozens of different wines bearing the same name, each one made by a different producer. And unlike Bordeaux, which recognizes its aristocracy by classifying individual estates like Château Talbot (Fourth Growth) and Château Montrose (Second Growth), but not the relative merits of their appellations (Saint-Julien and Saint-Estèphe, respectively), Burgundy formalizes a hierarchy of the places themselves, which is codified in the system of *Appellation Contrôlée*.

In addition to the variability inherent in a region where so many individual wines are made, what contributes to the frustration of many consumers in the export market is that so much of the red wine is damaged by heat in transport. No wine is more fragile—and more prone to damage by poor conditions in shipping and storage—than Pinot Noir from Burgundy. And who can blame wine buyers for complaining when fifty dollar wine tastes like dirty water out of a rusty bucket?

APPENDICES

PAIRING WINE WITH FOOD

ANTIPASTI: Prosecco di Valdobbiadene, Dolcetto d'Alba, Bardolino Chiaretto, or other Mediterranean white or rosé.

BBQ: Côtes du Rhône, Valpolicella, Dolcetto, Beaujolais.

BEANS: *As cassoulet, or bean stews with meat*: Southwest French reds like Cahors, Marcillac, and Gaillac.

BEEF: *Roasted*: Fine mature Burgundy or New World Pinot Noir. *Grilled*: New World Cabernet Sauvignon or Tuscan red like Chianti Riserva.

BOUILLABAISSE: Provence rosé.

CARPACCIO: Full fruity red wine, like Beaujolais. *If tuna*: Champagne rosé.

CHEESE: Old World cheeses are almost always successfully paired with wine that comes from the same place as the cheese, e.g.: Brie with Champagne; Muenster with Alsace Gewurztraminer; Roquefort with sweet white wine like Monbazillac or Sauternes; Asiago with Valpolicella; etc. Most mild hard cheeses are very good with moderately tannic red wine, and most full-flavored semi-soft or soft cheeses with aromatic dry or sweet white wines.

CHICKEN: *Roasted*: Full white Burgundy or New World Chardonnay. *Grilled*: Higher acid, aromatic white like unoaked Sauvignon Blanc, Vouvray, or Mediterranean rosé. Also, high acid, low tannin reds, including Provence, Barbera, Bardolino.

CHINESE: German Riesling, Pinot Noir, *jizake* (local sake).

CHOCOLATE: Banyuls, Port, Moscatello Sherry.

CORN ON THE COB: New World Chardonnay, Alsace Pinot Gris, Riesling.

CRAB: Fine German, Finger Lakes, or Anderson Valley Riesling.

DESSERTS: In general, wine is not easy to pair with dessert. Most sweet wines are much better with cheese. Try Moscato d'Asti for a refreshing accompaniment.

DUCK: Full-bodied reds, especially Bordeaux and Burgundy.

FISH AND SHELLFISH: *Raw*: Crisp whites like Chablis, Muscadet, dry German Riesling, unoaked Sauvignon Blanc and *jizake*(local sake). *Cooked*: Full-bodied whites like Vouvray, Verdicchio, Viognier, and white Burgundy with fat or oily fish or with sauces.

FOIE GRAS: Sweet white, like Sauternes, Monbazillac and Jurançon, or rich Alsace Pinot Gris, or Vouvray Moëlleux. Also, southwest French reds like Gaillac.

FONDUE: Chasselas from Savoie or Switzerland, or other straightforward fruity white.

GAME: Full-bodied reds.

GAZPACHO: Fino or Manzanilla Sherry.

GOAT CHEESE: Sauvignon Blanc, Vouvray.

GOOSE: Full bodied, not tannic red, or rich Riesling from Alsace.

HAM: Chinon or other middle Loire Cabernet Franc, Vouvray, Alsace or German Riesling.

JAMBALAYA: Loire Valley or New Zealand Sauvignon Blanc.

LAMB: Bordeaux and other southwest French reds, New World Cabernet Sauvignon, or Tuscan red like Chianti Riserva.

LASAGNA: Barbera d'Alba, Rosso Piceno or other low tannin, full red; also, as with other red-sauced pasta, Sauvignon Blanc.

LOBSTER: Condrieu or other Viognier, New World Chardonnay, Riesling Spätlese.

MOUSSAKA: Full-bodied Mediterranean reds, Zinfandel.

MUSHROOMS: Burgundy reds, New World Pinot Noir, Dolcetto, white Bordeaux (with a little oak), and right bank red Bordeaux.

OLIVES: Fino Sherry; or if olives are an important component of a dish, Southern Rhône, Provence, or other Mediterranean red or rosé.

OYSTERS: Chablis, dry Vouvray, Muscadet, Manzanilla Sherry.

PAELLA: Full-bodied rosé from Béarn, Irouléguy, Provence, or of course, Navarra.

PASTA: *With olive oil*: Unoaked crisp whites or Mediterranean rosé, or aromatic red like Ciro. *With seafood*: Verdicchio. *With cream*: Soave Classico, Riesling Kabinett, New World Chardonnay (not too oaky). *With tomato*: Unoaked Sauvignon Blanc, Barbera. *With meat*: Barbera, Montepulciano d'Abruzzo, or other rich, fruity red.

PÂTÉ: Fruity, low tannin reds, like Beaujolais, or rich, unoaked whites like Vouvray demi-sec or off-dry Riesling.

PESTO: Unoaked Sauvignon Blanc, Erbaluce, Arneis.

PIZZA: Barbera, Dolcetto, Montepulciano d'Abruzzo, or light-bodied Southern Rhônes. Also, Mediterranean rosés, and, as with red-sauced pasta, unoaked Sauvignon Blanc.

PORK: Vouvray, Pinot Blanc, Loire reds and Côtes du Rhône.

RABBIT: White Macon, or light-bodied Pinot Noir, Beaujolais, or Freisa d'Asti.

RISOTTO: Crisp aromatic whites like Nosiola, Pinot Bianco, Soave Classico. *With meat or mushrooms*: Dolcetto, Barbera, Freisa d'Asti, Valpolicella.

SALAD: Riesling Kabinett trocken, other very crisp, dry whites. (Be careful with the vinegar.)

SALMON: Aromatic whites like Sancerre (especially with sorrel sauce), Vouvray, New World Chardonay. Beaujolais (especially with grilled salmon), or fine Pinot Noir (especially with mushrooms).

SOUPS: Fortified whites like Sherry and Madiera, especially Manzanilla with chowders.

SUSHI: Vouvray, Verdicchio, Soave Classico, Albariño, German Riesling, or *jizake* (local sake).

TURKEY: Vouvray or off-dry Riesling.

VEAL: *With sauce*: fine mature red; or large-scaled white like Meursault.

VENISON: Northern Rhône reds, Tuscan and southwest French reds, and New World Cabernet Sauvignon and Zinfandel.

ZARUSOBA: Riesling kabinett, *jizake* (local sake).

GRAPE VARIETIES OF WINE

AMARONE: Corvina, Molinara, and Rondinella.

ANJOU ROUGE: Cabernet Sauvignon and Cabernet Franc.

BANDOL: Mourvèdre (minimum 50 percent), Grenache Noir, Syrah.

BANYULS: Grenache Noir.

BARBARESCO: Nebbiolo.

BARDOLINO: Corvina, Rondinella, and Molinara.

BAROLO: Nebbiolo.

BARSAC: As Sauternes. Sémillon, Sauvignon Blanc and Muscadelle.

BEAUJOLAIS: Gamay Noir.

BORDEAUX: *Red*: Merlot, Cabernet Sauvignon, Cabernet Franc, Malbec, Petit Verdot. *White*: Sauvignon Blanc, Sémillon, and Muscadelle.

BOURGUEIL: Cabernet Franc.

BRUNELLO DI MONTALCINO: Sangiovese.

BOURGOGNE (BURGUNDY): *Red*: Pinot Noir, (also Gamay Noir in Beaujolais). *White*: Chardonnay (also Aligoté when it appears on the label).

CAHORS: Malbec (minimum 70 percent), Tannat, and Merlot.

CARMIGNANO: Sangiovese and Cabernet Sauvignon.

CHABLIS: Chardonnay.

CHAMBERTIN: Pinot Noir.

CHAMBOLLE-MUSIGNY: Pinot Noir.

CHAMPAGNE: Pinot Noir, Pinot Meunier, and Chardonnay.

CHASSAGNE-MONTRACHET: Chardonnay.

CHÂTEAUNEUF DU PAPE: Thirteen varieties usually dominated by Grenache.

CHIANTI: Sangiovese with others.

CHINON: Cabernet Franc.

CONDRIEU: Viognier.

CORBIÈRES: Carignan (maximum 70 percent), Syrah, and others.

CORNAS: Syrah.

CORTON: Pinot Noir.

CORTON-CHARLEMAGNE: Chardonnay.

CÔTES DU RHÔNE: *Northern Reds*: Syrah. *Southern Reds*: Grenache and others. *Whites*: Viognier, Marsanne, Roussanne.

FENDANT: Chasselas (in Switzerland).

FINO SHERRY: Palomino Fino.

FRASCATI: Malvasia with Trebbiano.

GAILLAC: Duras and Braucol (Fer Servadou) with others, including Gamay Noir and Syrah.

GATTINARA: Nebbiolo.

GEVREY-CHAMBERTIN: Pinot Noir.

GIGONDAS: Grenache Noir and other Southern Rhône varieties.

GRAVES: *Red*: Cabernet Sauvignon, Merlot, and other Bordeaux red varieties. *White*: Sauvignon Blanc and Sémillon.

HERMITAGE: Syrah.

MÂCON: *White*: Chardonnay. *Red*: Pinot Noir.

MADEIRA: Sercial, Verdelho, Boal, and Malvasia.

MADIRAN: Tannat and the two Cabernets.

MANZANILLA: Palomino Fino.

MARCILLAC: Fer Servadou (locally called Mansois).

MÉDOC: Bordeaux varieties usually dominated by Cabernet Sauvignon.

MENETOU-SALON: Sauvignon Blanc.

MEURSAULT: Chardonnay.

MONTAGNY: Chardonnay.

MONTRACHET: Chardonnay.

MOULIN À VENT: Gamay Noir.

MUSCADET: Melon de Bourgogne.

NUITS-ST.-GEORGES: *Red*: Pinot Noir. *White*: Chardonnay or a clone of Pinot Noir giving white grapes.

ORVIETO: Trebbiano, Verdello, Grechetto, and Malvasia.

POMEROL: Merlot with Cabernet Franc.

POMMARD: Pinot Noir.

PORT: Touriga Nacional, Tinta Barroca, and at least eighty other varieties.

POUILLY-FUISSÉ: Chardonnay.

POUILLY-FUMÉ: Sauvignon Blanc.

PULIGNY-MONTRACHET: Chardonnay.

QUINCY: Sauvignon Blanc.

RIBERA DEL DUERO: Tempranillo (locally called Tinto Fino), and Cabernet Sauvignon.

RIOJA: Tempranillo and Garnacha (Grenache).

RUEDA: Verdejo and Viura.

SAINT-EMILION: Merlot with Cabernet Franc.

SALICE SALENTINO: Negroamaro and Malvasia Nera

SANCERRE: *White*: Sauvignon Blanc. *Red*: Pinot Noir.

SANTENAY: *Red*: Pinot Noir. *White*: Chardonnay.

SAUMUR-CHAMPIGNY: Cabernet Franc.

SAUTERNES: Sémillon with Sauvignon Blanc (a little Muscadelle is permitted).

SAVENNIÈRES: Chenin Blanc.

SHERRY: Palomino Fino, Pedro Ximénez, and Muscat of Alexandria.

SHIRAZ: Syrah (in Australia).

SOAVE: Garganega (minimum 70 percent) with Trebbiano di Soave, Pinot Bianco, and Chardonnay.

STEEN: Chenin Blanc (in South Africa).

TORGIANO: Sangiovese and Canaiolo Nero.

VACQUEYRAS: As Châteauneuf du Pape, with Grenache Noir usually dominating.

VALDEPEÑAS: Tempranillo (locally called Cencibel), sometimes with Airén.

VALPOLICELLA: Corvina, Molinara, and Rondinella.

VOLNAY: Pinot Noir

VOSNE-ROMANÉE: Pinot Noir.

VOUVRAY: Chenin Blanc.

GLOSSARY OF WINE WORDS

ACCESSIBLE: Subjective descriptor of a wine used when its characteristics can be easily perceived. Young wines that are more accessible than normally expected for their age are sometimes called **forward**.

ACETIC: Having the smell of vinegar (see **VA**).

ACIDITY: Important component of grapes that gives wine "crispness," mouth watering appeal, and contributes to "length" of finish and ageworthiness.

AOC: *Appellation d'Origine Contrôlée*. (see **appellation**).

APPELLATION: The name of the place of origin of a wine, by which it is identified, especially in France (see also **DOC, DOCG,** and **AVA**).

APPLEY: Having the smell of apples, as young Chardonnay, Mosel Riesling, and other white wines.

APRICOT: Smell associated with Riesling, especially in the Pfalz and in Alsace.

AROMA: The smells associated with the grape variety from which a wine is made and the fermentation process. Aroma is normally used to describe the smell of young wines.

ASTRINGENT: Wine that leaves the impression of dryness in the mouth as a result of the effect of its **tannin**.

ATTENUATED: A term to describe wine that tastes dilute, associated with over-cropped vines.

AUSLESE: Wine made in Germany from clusters of grapes that are individually selected for special characteristics, for example, clusters that have been infected with *Botrytis cinerea*. Auslese wines are usually made in a style that retains considerable **residual sugar**, but they may be vinified dry as well (see **trocken**).

AVA: American Viticultural Area, which roughly corresponds to **AOC**, but makes no restrictions on grape varieties or winemaking practices. Eighty-five percent of the grapes used to make a wine labeled with an AVA must come from the named region.

AZIENDA AGRICOLA: In Italy, a winery that makes wine from grapes grown in its own vine-yards.

AZIENDA VINICOLA: An Italian winery that purchases grapes or wine and bottles it under its own label.

BAKED: The smell of wine made from grapes grown in excessively hot conditions; alternatively, the sense of diminished freshness resulting from poor storage conditions.

BALANCE: Equilibrium of the major components in a wine, often specifically sweetness and acidity.

BARNYARD: The smell of hay and farm animals that is sometimes associated with old red Burgundy, southern Rhône, and Tuscan wines. Not always negative.

BARRIQUE: Oak barrel of approximately 225 liter capacity. Barriques are the barrels most commonly used to give oak flavor to wine.

BLACKCURRANT: The smell of these berries, also known as cassis, which is commonly noted in wines made from Cabernet Sauvignon, and sometimes Sauvignon Blanc.

BODY: The subjective impression of wine's alcoholic content plus its **extract**.

BOTRYTIS CINEREA: Fungus that grows on grapes, sometimes resulting in the disintegration of the skins, and the evaporation of water from the grapes, which can result in luscious sweet wines.

BOUQUET: The smell of wine that is bottle-aged, the result of complex organic reactions that take place over an extended period of time.

BREADY: The smell of freshly baked bread sometimes used to describe the smell of wines that are aged on their **lees**, especially Champagne.

BREATHING: The intentional exposure of wine to air for a period of time before drinking it, in the belief that it will become softer, and more mellow. Opening the bottle without pouring or decanting, however, has no effect, and is simply a pretentious habit.

BUTTERY: The attractive smell of fresh butter, usually associated with Chardonnay that has undergone **malolactic fermentation**.

CANTINA SOCIALE: An Italian co-operative winery.

CASCINA: Italian estate (literally, "farmhouse").

CEDAR: The cigar box smell associated with mature wines made from Cabernet Sauvignon, especially old wines from the Médoc. (It has nothing to do with the wooden barrels used in the wine-making, which are made of oak).

CELLARED AND BOTTLED: On California wine labels, means specifically that none of the wine was made at the winery where it was bottled.

CHAPTALISED: Wine made from juice to which sugar has been added in order to raise its alcoholic content (not to make it sweet).

CLASSICO: In Italy, the original center of a **DOC**, as Chianti Classico. It does not necessarily mean the best, or the most authentic (see **consorzio**).

CLIMAT: French term that incorporates all of the physical variables associated with a vineyard's location. In Burgundy, sometimes used interchangeably with other synonyms for vineyard.

CLOSED: Term to describe wine that is not **accessible** (see **dumb**).

CLOVE: Associated with new oak barrels, also sometimes with Pinot Noir.

CLOYING: Wine with sweetness that is not balanced with sufficient acidity.

COMPLEX: Having many different, well-integrated flavors.

CONSORZIO: Italian producers' trade association, as the Consorzio Chianti Classico, whose **Gallo Nero** (black rooster) seal on the necks of the bottles is erroneously believed to be a necessary mark of authenticity. In fact, it's nothing but the emblem of a club (which some of the best producers of Chianti Classico choose not to join).

CORKED: Tainted by the smell of TCA, which is formed when corks are infected with a common mold. Corked (sometimes, as "corky") wine smells musty, like wet cardboard in a damp basement.

CRISP: Wine with mouthwatering acidity.

CRU: "Growth," in the sense of a single vineyard, used especially when the vineyards are classified in a hierarchy, as *Cru Classé* and *Premier Cru*.

DOC: *Denominazione di Origine Controllata*, the Italian equivalent of the French **AOC** (also *Denominanação de Origem Controlada* in Portugal, and as DOCa, *Denominacíon de Origen Calificada* in Spain).

DOCG: *Denominazione de Origine Controllata e Garantita*, in Italy, the legal category established for the highest quality wines.

DOMAINE: In France, the collection of all the vineyard parcels owned, plus the winery, of a producer that grows its own grapes.

DUMB: Tasting term for young, concentrated wine that has little **nose**.

EISWEIN: Wine that is made from grapes that have frozen. Ice crystals are removed, and the remaining syrupy juice gives very sweet wine that retains **acidity**.

ESTATE-BOTTLED: Wine produced and bottled by the grower of the grapes. In California, both the vineyard and the winery must be located in the **AVA** that is named on the label.

EUCALYPTUS: Smell associated with Cabernet Sauvignon, especially wines from the Oakville-Rutherford **AVA** in Napa.

EXTRACT: The sum of all the non-volatile components of wine, which includes sugars, acids, minerals, **tannin**, pigments, and **glycerol**.

FATTORIA: Italian wine producing estate.

FINISH: The subjective impression a wine leaves on the senses after it is swallowed.

FIRM: The subjective impression that a wine has sufficient acidity.

FLORAL: Subjective descriptor of wine that smells of unspecified flowers.

FORWARD: The subjective sense that a wine is more mature than its age would suggest.

FRUIT: Non-phenolic and non-alcoholic **extract** plus the **aroma** of young wine that originates only from the grapes. Fruit is an important component of young wine, and is the component that "ripens" in ageworthy wines.

FRUITY: Wine with attractive **fruit**, sometimes erroneously used as a euphemism for "slightly sweet."

FULL-BODIED: Wine with a high concentration of alcohol and extract.

FÛTS DE CHÊNE: Oak barrels (French), sometimes seen on French wine labels to indicate that the wine was aged in barrels.

GLYCEROL: Byproduct of alcoholic fermentation and component of wine that has a sweet taste, and a slightly viscous texture. At the concentrations glycerol (or "glycerine") is present in wine, it makes no contribution to the apparent viscosity of the wine itself, and, contrary to popular belief, has nothing whatsoever to do with the phenomenon of **legs**.

GRAPEY: Wine that smells primarily of grapes.

GRASSY: The smell of cut grass, often associated with Sauvignon Blanc.

GROWN, PRODUCED, AND BOTTLED: On California labels means that 100 percent of the grapes used in a wine came from vineyards wholly controlled by the producing and bottling winery (see **estate-bottled**).

GUNFLINT: Smell of struck flint, common to Sauvignon Blanc wines from the Loire (sometimes "flinty").

GUTSABFÜLLUNG: In Germany, denotes estate-bottled.

HALBTROCKEN: In German, "half-dry." Halbtrocken wines contain between nine and eighteen grams per liter of residual sugar, which is usually balanced by high acidity. The indication is of the relative dryness of the finished wine, which is independent of its **prädikat** (see **QmP**).

HARD: Subjective descriptor of wine that is both **closed** and excessively tannic.

HERBACEOUS: The same as **grassy**, usually applied to red wines.

HOLLOW. Subjective descriptor for wine with alcohol and acid, but little other **extract** or **fruit**.

HOT: Excessively alcoholic.

IMBOTTIGLIATO ALL'ORIGINE: Estate-bottled Italian wine.

KABINETT: German **QmP** wine made from normally ripe grapes.

LANOLIN: Smell sometimes associated with Sémillon Blanc.

LEAD PENCIL: The smell of pencil shavings sometimes associated with Bordeaux, especially from the appellation Pauillac.

LEAN: Subjective descriptor of wine that is not full-bodied, but with other components in **balance**, not always negative.

LEES: The solid matter that precipitates out of fermenting wine, which includes dead yeast cells, grape fragments, and insoluble tartrates of acids, especially **potassium bitartrate**.

LEGS: The rivulets of wine that seem to climb up the inner surface of a swirled glass and then fall back into the liquid. Their width and number are often mistakenly taken as an indication of the wine's quality. However, they are simply an unreliable indicator of alcoholic strength.

LENGTH: Measure of the persistence of flavors after the wine is swallowed or spit out (see

finish).

LYCHEE: Smell associated with Gewurztraminer, especially in Alsace.

MADERIZED: Smelling like Madiera, the result of oxidation.

MALOLACTIC FERMENTATION: Secondary fermentation that results in the transformation of malic acid, which tastes sharp and tart, into lactic acid, which tastes soft and creamy. Always desirable in red wines, and contributes to the complexity of some white wines, especially barrel-fermented Chardonnay.

MEATY: As a textural descriptor, full-bodied. Also, aromatically, the butcher shop smell of meat, sometimes associated with wines from the southwest of France.

MINERAL: Subjective descriptor of wine that tastes of unspecified minerals. Associated with Mosel Riesling and Chablis.

MINT: Smell associated with Cabernet Sauvignon.

MIS EN BOUTEILLES AU DOMAINE: On French wine labels, indicates estate-bottled wine.

MOUTHFEEL: The sum of **tannin** and **body**. Mouthfeel is the tactile impression that wine makes inside the mouth.

MUSKY: Subjective descriptor of wine smells that have an exotic animal component.

MUST: Grape juice before fermentation.

MUSTY: The moldy, damp basement smell associated with **corked** wine. Not to be confused with **musky**.

NÉGOCIANT: French merchant producer, who buys grapes or wine and bottles it under his own label. As *négociant-éleveur*, it indicates that the négociant cares for and ages the wine before it is sold.

NOBLE ROT: (see *Botrytis cinerea*).

NOSE: The sum of **aroma** and **bouquet**.

OAKY: The smell of new oak barrels.

PETROL: Attractive smell mildly suggestive of kerosene or other petroleum distillate, associated with mature Riesling, especially from Germany.

PODERE: Small Italian estate.

POTASSIUM BITARTRATE: The potassium salt of tartaric acid, which forms crystals that are sometimes seen as a deposit in wine, or growing on the ends of corks. In white wines, novices sometimes mistake them for sugar, sometimes even for fragments of glass. In red wines they are often colored by the anthocyanins that give wine its color, and they appear as dark red crystals on the end of the cork. They are perfectly natural and harmless.

PRÄDIKAT: One of the indications of the ripeness the grapes that are used to make **QmP** German wines, as **kabinett**, **spätlese**, **auslese**, beerenauslese, **eiswein**, and trockenbeerenauslese.

PRODUTTORE: Italian wine producer. When seen on the label as *produttori* (plural), usually denotes a wine made by a co-operative.

PROPRIÉTAIRE: Proprietor (French). The owner of a vineyard.

RÉCOLTANT: French grape grower.

REDUCED: The smell associated with some red wines that are bottled too early, before they have incorporated sufficient oxygen. It results from the formation of hydrogen sulfide, which smells of rotten eggs.

REDUCTIVE: (see **reduced**).

ROSE PETAL: Smell associated with Gewurztraminer, especially from the Pfalz.

QbA: *Qualitätswein bestimmter Anbaugebiete*, the lower rank of quality German wine, which may be chaptalised. Finished QbA wines may be dry, as **trocken** or "half-dry," as **halbtrocken** wines, or they may contain more residual sugar.

QmP: *Qualitätswein mit Prädikat*, the higher rank of quality wine in Germany, graded according to the sugar content of the grapes at harvest, in ascending order as follows: **kabinett**, **spätlese**, **auslese**, beerenauslese, **eiswein**, and trockenbeerenauslese. QmP wines may not be **chaptalised**.

RESIDUAL SUGAR. Sugar that remains in wine after fermentation has ended. Depending on the grape variety and the **acidity**, residual sugar begins to be perceived as sweetness at concentrations as low as two to three grams per liter.

RISERVA: In Italy, a **DOC** wine that has been aged for a prescribed period of time at the winery before it is sold.

SHORT: The characteristic of wine with flavors that disappear quickly once the wine is swallowed (see **length** and **finish**).

SOFT: Low in **acidity**.

SPÄTLESE: German **QmP** wine made from late harvested grapes. Spätlese wines are not necessarily sweeter than **kabinett** wines (see **trocken**).

STEMMY: Descriptor of the hard, green taste of wine made with excessive contact with the stems of the grape clusters.

STRUCTURE: The sum of all of the tactile impression of a wine, including the effects of **tannin**, alcohol, acidity, **extract**, and sugar.

SULFITES: Negatively charged ions that result from the dissociation of sulfurous acid. They are a natural byproduct of fermentation, and are present in all wines, even those in which sulfur dioxide has not been used as an anti-oxidant. Sulfites are also present in high concentrations in fruit juices and dried fruits. They are completely harmless except to certain asthmatics, who may be profoundly allergic to them.

SULFURY: Smelling of sulfur. Wine usually loses the characteristic "burned match" smell of sulfur after it has been open for a while.

TANNIN: Phenolic wine component derived from the skins and seeds of grapes, and barrels in which wine ages. Tannin acts as a natural preservative in wine that is destined for long bottle age, and has the effect of making wine taste agreeably (or disagreeably) **astringent**.

TCA: Two, four, six-trichloroanisole, the **musty** smelling compound that results in **corked** wine.

TEARS: (see **legs**).

TERROIR: French term that encapsulates all of the physical characteristics of vineyards that may influence how wine made from their grapes will taste. Also as "*goût de terroir*," the particular flavor of a distinctive wine, sometimes earthy and rustic.

TOBACCO: The smell of fresh cigarette tobacco sometimes associated with red Bordeaux (especially Graves) and some mature red wines made from Tempranillo.

TROCKEN: Dry (German). Trocken wines contain less than nine grams per liter of residual sugar. The indication is of the finished wine's dryness, which is independent of its **prädikat**. There are even **auslese** wines that are labeled "trocken." (see **QmP**).

TRUFFLE: Smell associated with some Piemontese wines made from Nebbiolo. Also, as white truffle, sometimes used interchangeably with **petrol** to describe an attractive component of the smell of mature Riesling.

VA: Volatile acidity, normally used in reference to acetic acid, which is the most common volatile acid in wine. At concentrations above one gram per liter, wine may begin to smell of vinegar.

VANILLA: Smell associated with new oak barrels, especially of American oak.

VARIETAL: Wine made from (or named for) a single grape variety. In California, varietal wine must contain at least 75 percent of the named variety.

VELVETY: Textural descriptor for wines with fine **tannin**.

VENDEMMIA: Harvest, as in "vintage" (Italian).

VIGNA, VIGNETO: A single vineyard (Italian).

VIGNAIOLO: Italian grape grower.

VIGNERON: French grape grower.

VINTED AND BOTTLED: Like **cellared and bottled**, means that none of the wine was made by the winery that bottled it.

VITICOLTORE: Italian grape grower.

VITICULTEUR: French grape grower.

WEEDY. (see **herbaceous**).

WEINGUT: German wine growing estate.

WEINKELLEREI: German winery that buys in grapes or wine, but does not own vineyards.

WOODY: Wine in which the smell of oak overwhelms the **fruit**. Also sometimes used to describe the smell of dirty barrels.

BIBLIOGRAPHY

Anderson, Burton. *Vino*. Boston: Little Brown & Co., 1980.

Anderson, Burton. *The Wine Atlas of Italy*. New York: Simon & Schuster, 1990.

Belfrage, Nicolas. *Life Beyond Lambrusco*. London: Sidgwick & Jackson, 1985.

Darlington, David. *Angel's Visits: An Inquiry Into the Mystery of Zinfandel*. New York: Henry Holt, 1991.

Duijker, Hubrecht, and Michael Broadbent. *The Bordeaux Atlas and Encyclopaedia of Châteaux*. New York: St. Martin's Press, 1997.

Friedrich, Jacqueline. *A Wine and Food Guide to the Loire*. New York: Henry Holt & Co.,1996.

George, Rosemary. *The Country Wines of France*. London: Faber and Faber, 1990.

Gleave, David. *The Wines of Italy*. London: Salamander Books, 1989.

Jamieson, Ian. *German Wines*. London: Faber and Faber, 1991.

Kramer, Matt. *Making Sense of Wine*. New York: William Morrow & Co., 1989.

Kramer, Matt. *Making Sense of Burgundy*. New York: William Morrow & Co., 1990.

Kramer, Matt. *Making Sense of California Wine*. New York: William Morrow & Co., 1992.

Livingstone-Learmonth, John. *The Wines of the Rhône*. London: Faber & Faber, 1991.

Norman, Remington. *The Great Domaines of Burgundy*. New York: Holt & Co., 1993.

Peynaud, Emile. *The Taste of Wine*. London: Macdonald & Co., Ltd., 1987.

Pigott, Stuart. *Life Beyond Liebfraumilch*. London: Sidgwick & Jackson, 1988.

Pigott, Stuart. *The Wine Atlas of Germany*. Edited by Hugh Johnson. London: Mitchell Beazley, 1995.

Robinson, Jancis. *Vines Grapes and Wine*. New York: Alfred A. Knopf, 1986.

Robinson, Jancis, ed. *The Oxford Companion to Wine*. Oxford: Oxford University Press, 1994.

Robinson, Jancis. *Guide to Wine Grapes*. Oxford: Oxford University Press, 1996.

Robinson, Jancis. *How to Taste*. New York: Simon & Schuster, 2000.

Sharp, Andrew. *Winetaster's Secrets*. Toronto: Warwick Publishing, 1996.

Simon, Joanna. *Wine With Food*. New York: Simon & Schuster, 1996.

Spurrier, Steven. *Académie du Vin Guide to French Wines*. New York: Mitchell Beazley Publishers, 1991.

Stevenson, Tom. *The Wines of Alsace*. London: Faber & Faber Ltd., 1993.

Strang, Paul. *Wines of South-West France*. London: Kyle Cathie Ltd., 1996.

Thompson, Bob. *The Wine Atlas of California and the Pacific Northwest*. New York: Simon & Schuster 1993.

144

ABOUT THE AUTHOR

Greg Moore co-owns the Moore Brothers Wine Company, named Best New Wine Shop by *Food & Wine* magazine. For nearly twenty years, he was the sommelier at Philadelphia's renowned Le Bec-Fin.